THE SCOTTISH MINISTERS'
WIDOWS' FUND
1743-1993

THE SCOTTISH MINISTERS' WIDOWS' FUND

1743-1993

Edited by A Ian Dunlop

SAINT ANDREW PRESS

EDINBURGH

First published in 1992 by
SAINT ANDREW PRESS
121 George Street, Edinburgh EH2 4YN
on behalf of
The Churches and Universities (Scotland)
Widows' and Orphans' Fund

ISBN 0 86153 153 1

British Library Cataloguing in Publication Data
A catalogue record for this book is
available from the British Library.

ISBN 0-86153-153-1

This book has been set in 11/12 pt Times

Cover design by Mark Blackadder
Cover photograph by Walter Bell
Typeset by J & L Composition Ltd, Filey, North Yorkshire
Printed and bound by Athenaeum Press Ltd, Newcastle upon Tyne

CONTENTS

DISRUPTION TO AMALGAMATION
1843-1930

SINCE 1930
The Churches and Universities (Scotland) Widows' and Orphans' Fund

APPENDICES

NOTES ON CONTRIBUTORS

The Late Rev. William Cameron MA BD was a minister of the Free Church of Scotland. He was appointed to Burghhead in 1932 and Buccleuch, Edinburgh in 1950. In 1953 he was appointed Professor of Greek and New Testament and in 1973 Principal of the Free Church College. He was also Clerk to the General Assembly and twice Moderator—in 1962 and 1977. He became a Trustee of the Fund in 1953 and a member of the Finance Committee in 1967. He very kindly agreed to write for this book the History of the Widows' Funds in the Free Church after the Disruption and in Secession Churches. When, sadly, Mr Cameron died in 1990, his recently completed paper was lying on his desk.

The Late James Bremner Dow MA FFA was an Actuary with Standard Life who became a greatly valued Trustee of the Widows' Fund in 1961. Appointed to the Finance Committee, he became its Convener from 1974-1982. He died in 1987. He gave the paper which is printed in this book as a lecture to the Faculty of Actuaries on 16 October 1972. It gave rise to good discussion and was published in the Faculty's Transactions as part 3 of volume 33.

FOREWORD

I was delighted to accept an invitation to write a short Foreword to this volume of papers on the establishment and subsequent history over the past two hundred and fifty years of the Churches and Universities (Scotland) Widows' and Orphans' Fund.

I know that it will be of great interest to all and of considerable value to historians and actuaries. I do not think it is generally known that the work of Robert Wallace and Colin Maclaurin in the early 1740s represents the first recorded development of actuarial thought in Scotland. It was of course due to their work, and to the energies of Alexander Webster, that the Fund can lay claim to being the first to be established on what are known today as actuarial principles. I find it remarkable that all this occurred some eighty-two years before my own company, Standard Life, began its business in Edinburgh.

Standard Life is delighted to have helped with the publication of this volume. Our association with the Fund extends as far back as 1849 when our then manager, W T Thomson, carried out the first Report into its finances since the Disruption. It has been continued by A E King in his capacity as Actuary some fifty years ago, by J B Dow as a Trustee for over 25 years, and of course by G C Philip who is the Fund's present Actuary.

I hope you will enjoy the volume as much as I did.

A S Bell
Managing Director
Standard Life

COMMENDATION
FROM THE CHURCHES

This volume tells how the Church of Scotland, two hundred and fifty years ago, solved a very practical problem and showed the world how to walk in the ways of Life and Annuity Insurance.

We commend it to those interested in the history of the Church and those concerned with finance and insurance at home and abroad.

James L Weatherhead
Principal Clerk
General Assembly of the Church of Scotland

Clement Graham
Principal Clerk
General Assembly of the Free Church of Scotland

INTRODUCTION

The Trustees of the Fund feel that notice should be taken of
the fact that Two Hundred and Fifty Years will have passed
in 1993 since the General Assembly of the Church of
Scotland approved a scheme for a Widows' and Orphans'
Fund for their ministers, and that, in part celebration of the
completion of a quarter-millenium, a volume should be
prepared recording something of the life and work of the
Fund during these years. It will be seen that this is a
somewhat special fund for it can claim to be the earliest
scheme of its kind. In 1744 the Royal Assent was given to an
Act of Parliament which gave the fund all the authority of
law and made it compulsory for all future ministers of the
Church of Scotland to join.

In the *First Book of Discipline* (as reported in Knox's
History), prepared at the time of the Reformation in 1560,
there is a note: "provision for the Wyffis of ministerss after
their deceise to be remittet to the discretioun of the Kirk."
The Kirk, however, failed to obtain the pre-Reformation
church wealth, even to pay its ministers and it took many
years before the ministers could be expected to make
provision for a pension for their widows. In 1742, three
ministers of Edinburgh, after several attempts had been
made to deal with the problem and before there was much
guidance for them, prepared a scheme, had their calculations checked by Colin Maclaurin, the Professor of
Mathematics in Edinburgh, had it approved by the General
Assembly and applied for the Act of Parliament.

Other acts were necessary in due course to deal with

minor errors and changing circumstances but still the Fund provides for the widows and fatherless children of ministers of the Church of Scotland, the Free Church of Scotland and some of the professors of the four old Scottish Universities, although no new professors have been admitted to the Fund since 1966.

It is thought that the following papers will be of interest to ministers, actuaries, historians and many others. The Fund is peculiarly Scottish, created by men of character and foresight, who were not afraid to venture into unknown areas of finance as their brothers did into unknown parts of the world. These men were, too, in the forefront of the Enlightenment in every area of human thought. Their work ought to be acknowledged and praised.

Some of the essays in this volume are reprinted, with permission, from publications of recent years. Some have been specially prepared. In the nature of things, then, some repetition is unavoidable.

The history of the Fund is broken into three parts. In 1843 a large secession from the Church of Scotland took place with the creation of The Free Church of Scotland, which formed its own Fund for its own new ministers. In 1930, after the Union of The United Free Church and the Church of Scotland in 1929, the present Fund was formed by an amalgamation of both the existing funds.

In recent years, the Churches have also been providing non-contributory pensions to widows of ministers. It should be noted too that, from the beginning, professors in the old Scottish Universities, who had to sign the formula of acceptance of the Reformed Faith, asked to be admitted to the Fund (and Parliament granted their request). Recently, however, since the universities made their own provision for widows, no more professors were admitted, though those who were members continued their membership.

The Trustees wish to express thanks to those who have contributed papers, especially Mr George C Philip, the Fund's actuary and Drs W F Scott and D J P Hare, two actuaries who have examined the claim that the Fund is the earliest actuarially-based Fund in the world. Mr J B Dow, an actuary with Standard Life and a very active Trustee

(1961–87), died some years ago and Principal Cameron of the Free Church (a Trustee from 1967) died in 1990, leaving his article on the Free Church Scheme on his desk.

We are grateful to Mr J S Ritchie for summarising the Acts of Parliament, and to the Rev. D H Whiteford and all who have read proofs and given encouragement.

The Editor wishes to thank Miss Lesley A Taylor and Mr Derek Auld of Saint Andrew Press for their advice, patience and courtesy.

The Trustees would record their gratitude to the Scottish Mutual Assurance Society and their deep appreciation of the very generous gift from the Standard Life which has made this publication possible.

A Ian Dunlop
Editor

THE FIRST
HUNDRED YEARS
1743 - 1843

CHAPTER 1

Provision for Ministers' Widows in Scotland —Eighteenth Century*

A Ian Dunlop TD MA BD

From the time of the Reformation in 1560 it was necessary to do something about immediate provision for the widows of ministers suddenly having to leave manse and glebe, some-times with young children, and it was reasonable that the fruits of the benefice during at least part of the vacancy should go to the widow. This becomes legalised in the Law of Ann and in due course was regulated by Act of Parliament 1672 (Ch. II, 2nd Parl. 3rd Sess. c. 13). As a rule, the stipend for the half-year during which the minister died was paid, one half to the widow and the other half, in equal shares, to the children surviving the minister. When there was no widow, all went to the children. Section 9 of the 1925 Act ended these payments for widows of ministers admitted after the Act and one year after the standardisation of stipend. The United Free Church had paid Widows' Grants (£60 in 1920) and the Church of Scotland began the same practice where there was no Ann. In 1950 the payment was £100, in 1960 £150. Also in some cases there was a next-of-kin grant if there was no widow.

However Ann was a once-and-for-all payment and did not provide for the continued upkeep of widows, and one wonders how in the early days they were able to live at all. Some remarried and some were cared for out of session Poor Funds.[1] There was a certain amount of concern, and bequests were sometimes made for them. For example in the will of Dr Alexander Burnett, Archbishop of St Andrews, who died in 1684, there were bequests of 300 merks to two widows and 200 to two others and "if any of them die before their legacies

3

are due, the forementioned sums to be paid to the Archbishop
of Glasgow and the Bishop of Edinburgh to be given to other
relicts of ministers whom they judge most necessitous."[2]

It will be of interest to look at one early provision for
widows, the so-called Centesima Fund, which still exists and
is administered by the Trustees of the present Fund. On
20th June 1688, a bond was taken out, in the names of
Alexander, Bishop of Edinburgh and Robert Scott, Dean of
Glasgow, with the Burgh of Edinburgh for 7,615 merks, the
interest to be for "the relicts and orphans" of 31 ministers of
the diocese of Edinburgh. The money must have been raised
by 1685, for Andrew Cant of the High Kirk in Edinburgh,
one of the 31, died in December of that year. Nearly all the
31, including Rose, were deprived by 1691. The interest
accumulated and by 1712 the principal and interest amounted
to "11,809.11.11 pounds" (Scots). The Synod of Lothian in
that year began a process before the Lords of Council and
Session claiming the right of administration because of the
abolition of prelacy. The matter was settled by all parties
and it was agreed that £5,142 of the sum be handed to the
Bishop of Edinburgh and the episcopal ministers, and the
balance of 10,000 merks be allowed to accumulate, the
interest to be given to the widows and orphans in the first
degree of the contributors while any such live. Thereafter
the right of applying the interest would devolve on modera-
tors of the several presbyteries of the diocese of Edinburgh
as bounded in 1688, and to the Principal and professors of
Divinity of the College of Edinburgh for the time being and
their successors in office, for the benefit of relicts and
orphans of episcopal ministers of the diocese of Edinburgh
so long as any of them are alive, and thereafter the benefits
should pass to the relicts and orphans of any minister of the
area of the old diocese. The bond must not be uplifted or
disturbed without the consent of at least two of the Lords of
Session. The minutes of the trustees begin in 1784 and make
interesting reading. Principal Robertson was in the chair at
the second meeting and Dr Hunter agreed to act as factor.
Mrs Pollock, the daughter of Adam Waddell of Whitsome,
one of the original contributors and the only person alive
having a right to the benefit on the original terms, died in

1789 and it was agreed to pay the interest to necessitous children of ministers in the diocese area who had not contributed to the Widows' Fund. Sir Henry Moncrieff, the collector, provided names appropriate. In 1825 Principal Baird was in the chair and it was reported that since 1803 it had been impossible to find anyone suitable to enjoy the money and £450 had accumulated.

In 1829 the clerk's affairs became embarrassed and although the bond was intact it looks as if about £500 disappeared, even if for a while the interest on it was made available for payments to orphans. Dr Chalmers took a hand when he became Professor of Divinity but it seems to have been difficult to get proper attendance of managers or committee at the time of the Synod meeting. In 1835 the interest fell from £40 per annum in consequence of the City of Edinburgh's financial situation and in 1836 the city was only able to pay 15/– in the pound with interest at 4% until paid up.

Principal Baird was now old and unable to keep an eye on things so that nothing happened until 1838 when notice was sent to Mr Young, the agent of the Church, requesting him to call for the unpaid dividends of the Centesima Fund. The Rev Dr Muir, Moderator of the General Assembly made enquiry as to the purposes of the Fund and a deposit receipt for £106.12/– was obtained from the British Linen Company Bank in the names of Dr Muir and the Moderator of the Presbytery of Edinburgh. The principal was now £505 and new bonds were prepared for £100 each.

In 1842 Principal Lee took a hand and tidied up arrangements. The agent of the Church became secretary and treasurer and for many years an annual report was made to the General Assembly. In 1851 it was agreed, quite incorrectly, to make payments to the Misses May and Ann Morison, whose father was the composer of paraphrases, and who had lost their whole substance in the failure of the Aberdeen Bank.

Since then the annuities have been paid regularly to ladies whose parents or husbands have been ministers in the area of the former diocese of Edinburgh and the capital has been increased by reinvestment and capitalising of surplus income.[3]

But let us return to the more general provision for widows and orphans. Credit for first suggesting, in 1716, a fund for widows is given to Patrick Cowper, minister of Pittenween, born in 1660 and much persecuted in the Second Episcopacy. He spent time in Holland and after the Toleration was ordained in the meeting-house at Bannockburn. He died in 1740.

Several attempts were made in the next quarter-century to make provision on a voluntary basis and remove the scandal of ministers' widows living in destitution. In 1718 the General Assembly passed an Act[4] and Recommendation concerning a fund for "maintaining the Indigent Widows and Orphans of ministers." This is a carefully prepared Act, recommending every minister to give a tenth of his stipend for one year to the Moderator of Presbytery who would hand it to a responsible person appointed by the Synod. Newly appointed ministers should elect to join within two years of admission. The money collected should be turned into stock, the interest from which should benefit widows and orphans of contributors. The maximum benefit would be £10 sterling per annum payable at the time of the Synod meeting. Any surplus would be capitalised. Management would be in the hands of the contributors and any charitably disposed persons who contributed more than £10 sterling. Provision was made for appointing a committee in the Synod. Such presbyteries as might have already made provision for widows, could phase their schemes into the new one.

In 1723 some contributors in the Synod of Lothian drew the attention of the General Assembly to the fact that a number of ministers had neglected to pay the tenth of stipend by the last date permitted in the 1718 Act and now wished to contribute. The General Assembly passed an Act[5] extending the time to Whitsunday 1725, interest from the time when it should have been paid being added to the payment due.

It appears that sometime after 1723 there was put forward the idea of a general fund, in place of synodical funds, to be managed by the General Assembly or their deputies, for in 1735 the Assembly, in a new Act,[6] referred to this idea and considered that its existence had militated against the success of the synodical funds. There would be "great difficulties which would necessarily occur in raising and managing the more general fund, and there being now no prospect of any success in the said scheme for a general fund, the General Assembly considered that their synodical scheme should be adhered to and vigorously advanced, and again extended the date by which ministers might join, to Whitsunday 1736, subject to the agreement of the contributors and payment of interest from the time when payment should have been made."

It would be valuable to know more about the proportion of ministers who joined the synodical scheme and how it operated. And were the statistics available to those who instigated what became the Widows' Fund? In any case it appears that the synodical schemes failed and "proved ineffectual because of their limited nature and from want of a common rule and proper authority to enforce them."[7] It had become necessary to take a collection in the Assembly House each year for the relicts or children of ministers.[8] The widows had been receiving out of public charity.

According to the *Fasti*,[9] the first move for a Widows' Fund is said to have been made by John Mathison, minister of the High Kirk, Edinburgh 1710–52, in 1741, but the Act of 1735 indicates that the matter was being discussed before then and it is difficult now to assess the credit properly. It seems certain that it was primarily the work of a group of the burgh ministers of the City of Edinburgh. The credit usually goes to Alexander Webster, ordained in 1733 and admitted to Tolbooth, Edinburgh, where his father had been minister, in 1737. Like his father and his brother-in-law, Ebenezer Erskine, he was an ardent evangelical and drew packed congregations at the Tolbooth Kirk. He was at the same time a man of notoriously convivial habits and perhaps therefore of great popularity. It looks as if Webster collected the data and provided the impetus for action.[10] The other name principally involved was Robert Wallace, minister of New North, Edinburgh, from 1738. Wallace was born in 1696 or 1697, admitted to Moffat in 1723 and New Greyfriars in 1733. Before ordination he had assisted James Gregory,

Professor of Mathematics in Edinburgh; he helped to found the Rankenian Club in 1717 and also the Philosophical Society which became The Royal Society of Edinburgh in 1783. He was in disfavour during Walpole's time, partly because he refused to read the proclamation after the Porteous Riot, but after Walpole was removed in 1742 he was entrusted with the management of Church business and patronage matters in Scotland and he was strategically placed for action on behalf of widows. Perhaps his interest in widows meant that he did not work for the abolition of the Patronage Act and it is certain that when writing to presbytery members about patronage matters he took occasion to stimulate interest in the widows' scheme.[11] He was a skilled mathematician and did many of the calculations as to life probability, value of annuities, etc.[12]

The other person involved was George Wishart, minister of Tron, Edinburgh. He was ordained to St Cuthbert's Edinburgh in 1726 and succeeded his father, Principal Wishart in the Tron in 1730. He was deeply respected as a preacher, became Principal Clerk of Assembly in 1746, was Moderator in 1748 and died full of years in 1785.

At the time of the General Assembly in 1742 a definite move was made to establish a general fund and, perhaps because Webster was not a member in 1742, a special meeting of the Committee on Overtures was called for the evening of Saturday 8th May, "for receiving any schemes or proposals that may be offered for raising a Fund for widows of ministers. Any member of Assembly or minister of this church may be heard."[13] Statistics from all the presbyteries, except two or three, were presented showing figures from 1st March 1722—how many had died, how many had left widows, how many widows were still in life and how many remained unmarried. The promoters, Webster and Wallace, had had to collect the information and work out a scheme without the aid of mortality tables. All that was available was the evidence of the Breslau registers contained in Halley's Tables of 1693. The first figures were inaccurate but it was thought that 27 ministers died yearly on average, of whom 18 left widows. There were 304 widows widowed since 1722 of whom 280 were still unmarried and it was considered that 300 would be the maximum in life at any time. Since Ann and stipend arrears could provide for the first year, the number to be cared for could be reduced to 261.

The plan put, presumably by Webster and Wallace, before the Committee of Overtures was for "the establishing of a fund by Act of Parliament for an annuity to the widow of every minister and a stock to the children of such as should leave no widow, founded on an annual tax payable out of their benefices and a capital arising from the surpluses of these taxes during the earlier years of the scheme when there would be no great burden on the fund; and as the ministers happening to die soonest would have paid least into the common stock, the provisions of widows and children were to be small at the beginning and to bear a growing proportion to the sums contributed by their husbands and fathers."[14]

However, some members of the committee criticised the scheme because it would not quickly enough relieve the indigent and necessitous, and the prospect of managing a capital sum presented great difficulties to their minds.[15] Another scheme, presumably also prepared beforehand, was substituted, without a capital sum and with no provision for children. And this was put to the Assembly on Friday 14th May. The annuity was to be £20 and the trustees were to assess every stipend annually, whether occupied or vacant "in an equal sum not exceeding £4 Stg." When these payments were not enough, a sum of up to £20 once and for all would be called for from those first ordained or admitted in the previous year. If this were still insufficient a graduated levy would be imposed on ministers with the highest stipends. The assessments were to be gathered by presbytery collectors who would pay over to a general collector between Whitsunday and Martinmas. The general collector would pay the widows on a presbyterial certificate in Edinburgh at Martinmas. Expenses of management, determined by the Assembly, were to be covered. The ministers of Edinburgh, the quorum being nine, would be the trustees, accountable to the Assembly. If a minister demitted or were deposed and continued to pay, his widow would benefit. It was considered that existing presbytery and Synod funds could be used for children.

The 1742 Assembly sent this scheme for consideration by Presbyteries and report to the November Commission. Detailed instructions were given about voting in presbytery, dissenters to be named. Non-reply by presbytery was to be taken as concurrence. The Commission was given power, if there were a majority of ministers in favour, to petition the King and Parliament for an Act. The overture and scheme was accompanied by Reasons in Support, drawn up by a Committee appointed for the purpose.

When the Commission met in November 1742 it was found that 600 ministers, about two-thirds, approved the scheme in principle, but most presbyteries suggested altera-tions. The tax on entrants would be too heavy, the present incumbents had too great an advantage and no provision had been made for orphans.[16] Webster wrote later that almost all presbyteries insisted that a capital should be created so that future entrants should not be taxed higher than present incumbents. Some suggested delay and in some cases no report had been made or information was insufficient. A committee of seven was appointed and all ministers invited to join with the committee to consider the replies and revise the scheme so that the presbyteries could reconsider things and report to the March Commission. The result was that bit by bit Wallace and Webster seem to have been able to persuade committee and presbyteries to return to their original scheme with one noticeable difference—that "the provisions of families of such ministers as should die soonest, even in the first year of the scheme . . . were to be as great as the provisions of those who should live longest."[17] Wallace was able to point out that without the creation of a stock, bearing interest, the payment required from new entrants would be an intolerable proportion of stipend from about the sixteenth year of the fund's operation.

Robert Wallace was Moderator of the 1743 Assembly and the revised scheme was considered by a committee of the whole House and with more alterations reported to the General Assembly. It was approved and arrangements made to request an Act of Parliament, with the proviso that taxes were not to exceed the sums mentioned nor the produce of them used for any purpose other than those proposed. The Principal and professors of the University of Edinburgh petitioned to be allowed to be covered by the scheme and the Assembly agreed and also that professors in other universities might do likewise.

Immediately after the Assembly, it appears that Wallace sent a copy of the scheme to Colin Maclaurin, Professor of Mathematics at Edinburgh, the celebrated mathematician with a European reputation who was to die in 1746 as a result of exposure when evading the Highland rebels. Maclaurin may have been acting on behalf of the Edinburgh professors and he replied that it was "so good that minute observations against the absolute perfection of the scheme seem to be improper." However, he was mildly critical, as indeed Wallace and Webster still were. He was "apprehensive that the capital will not rise so fast as is supposed without deductions from provisions for the children." Also he thought it "remarkably advantageous for those ministers advanced in years."[18] There is a paper headed "Tables of Widows' Scheme 1743" and marked "I think they were made by Mr Colin Maclaurin", showing progress of the scheme according to the doctrine of chances. In the first table, if a marriage tax equal to the premium be paid, the stock would reach a maximum of £32,974 after 24 years. In the second, if marriage tax be paid and children receive half provision for the first five years and three-quarters for the next five years and widows have no annuity in the first year, the stock would be £47,145 at 24 years and still be increasing.[19] Wallace also signed a printed memorial on the merits of the scheme, which was circulated in July.

The scheme had to be put into the more precise parliamentary form and language and some minor changes were necessary in content, for example because Edinburgh Presbytery wished other trustees in addition to their own ministers to be appointed. The Commission, meeting in November, received requests from Glasgow and St Andrews professors to join the fund and appointed Robert Wallace and George Wishart to go to the Parliament in London and apply for an Act. The Bill was drawn up by Adam Anderson and revised by Sir Dudley Rider, the Attorney General. The Lord Advocate too was much involved—he drew up the first draft of the Bill—and the Commissioners took care to gain the support of the Scottish members by interview and letter. The time was ripe, for Wallace's reputation stood high with the Government, even if there were suspicions of the loyalty of the Highland areas. One wonders what would have happened had things been delayed for two years.

While in London the two ministers received a number of letters from the committee in Edinburgh asking for information and making suggestions, and they must have annoyed the committee by their evasive replies. There is a comment in Wallace's hand on the letters: "When they were in London several peevish and unwise orders were sent them and they learned by experience how difficult it was to be directed and advised by a Committee at Edinburgh".[20] They took time off and had to apologise for absence from the first meeting of the trustees, on 10th April, after the passing of the Act. The Bill, promoted by the Scots members was little changed in the Commons and Lords and received the Royal Assent on 2nd March 1744 as 17 Geo. II cap 11. It was to take effect on 25th March 1744.

The provisions of the Act may be summarised. All ministers and professors admitted before 25th March 1744 had the option to join; all admitted subsequently were required to do so and choose to pay one of the four rates (146 declined and the last died in 1800). The annual rates were £2 12s. 6d., £3 18s. 9d., £5 5s. and £6. 11s. 3d. The corresponding annuities were £10, £15, £20 and £25. Children would receive £100, £150, £200 and £250 single payments divided equally among them, i.e. equal to ten years' widow's annuities; and if the widow died or remarried within ten years then the child or children would receive a sum which would make up ten years' annuities. In default of choosing a rate, the second rate would be fixed. After expenses of management, not more than £250 per annum, the surplus funds would be lent compulsorily to principals, professors and ministers in a set order of presbyteries in sums of £30. The £30 was on a bond and repayable on death, and the minister or professor had to pay interest at 4%. This may seem a curious way of investing the money as it accumulated but some young ministers must have been glad to have the use of £30 in their early years. Capital in addition to this might be accumulated to the limit of £35,000, any surpluses thereafter to be distributed proportionately to children entitled in the year to receive provision. If in any year the income fell short of expenditure and payments, the widows and children were to suffer deduction proportionately in that year, and to be repaid out of surpluses in later years; the accumulation of capital was not to suffer. Marriage tax equal to one year's rate was to be paid unless the lady were a widow entitled to an annuity. Vacant stipends and salaries were subject to tax of £3 2s. for each half-year or £2 10s. if the former incumbent had not received the £30 loan. Dates of payment were carefully laid down, later dates being provided for ministers in the Western Isles. The trustees were to be the ministers of the Presbytery of Edinburgh and the Principal and professors of the University of Edinburgh and also two appointed by the other universities and one from each presbytery annually. Those elected annually might decline. In addition all ministers, "in any of the presbytery-seats of Scotland", and professors were appointed trustees unless they declined in due form within six months of appointment. The quorum was nine and there were to be four stated meetings per year. Absentees paid £1 unless they had reasonable excuse accepted. The General Assembly would appoint the collector and the trustees a clerk. The collector must give a bond for £7,000 and he would receive a salary of £155 per annum. Instructions were given for the provision of proper information and list by presbyteries, with monetary penalty for failure. An annual report was to be made to the General Assembly.

The committee appointed to consider the Act reported to the General Assembly of 1744 that the Act had been passed. The Lord Advocate, the Chancellor and the Speaker of the Parliament were thanked for their help, then Wallace and Wishart for all they had done. Webster was congratulated for "his extraordinary pains in the rise and progress of the scheme." Petitions were received from the professors of

King's and Marischal Colleges in Aberdeen to join. Those of Marischal were accepted and also King's after a debate and decision to sustain a request made at a meeting of professors by casting vote. The Assembly passed an Act ordering the presbyteries to keep necessary records.[21] The costs of the commissioners in London amounting to £500 were ordered to be paid out of the Church's public fund. It was ruled that the minister of the Castle of Edinburgh was not eligible to join. Mr James Stewart, Attorney in Exchequer, was appointed as Collector-General and a bond arranged.

From the time the trustees first met, Webster was the active leader and Wallace seems to have taken little direct part beyond attending meetings. In 1744 he was appointed a Chaplain to the King and a Dean of the Chapels Royal and in 1759 was given a DD from Edinburgh University. He died in 1771. Shortly after the 1744 Act was passed he gave his attention to writing *A Dissertation on the Numbers of Mankind* for the Philosophical Society. This was published in 1753 and was translated into French together with a paper by Hume *On The Populousness of Ancient Nations!* Wallace was an early moderate but never an extreme one, even if he did write an essay on *The Principles and the Art of Dancing.*[22] His *Various Prospects of Mankind, Nature and Providence*, 1761, in a sense forestalled Malthus and was referred to by Hazlitt. Much of his writing was never published.

Webster was to go on with his statistical labours and, at the instigation of the Government, take the first census of Scotland in 1755.[23] Edinburgh made him a Doctor of Divinity in 1760 and he became a Royal Chaplain and a Dean of the Chapels Royal. He is credited with suggesting the creation of the New Town of Edinburgh. He succeeded Stewart as general collector of the Widows' Fund in 1771 and he died in 1784.

In 1745, at the General Assembly, it was reported that there were 942 benefices with 897 ministers and 69 university appointments with 65 filled; 31 had paid at the lowest rate, 201 at the next, 338 the next and 248 the highest, between 25th March 1744 and Martinmas 1745; 16 ministers had died and six widows and one family had come on the fund, one widow receiving £15, four £20 and one £25. By 14th May 1745, £7,380 had been ordered to be lent in £30 lots.[24] It appeared already that older men were choosing the higher rates.[25] The Assembly approved an Act[26] giving detailed instructions about certificates and the manner of keeping registers.

However, the trustees became exasperated at the inaccuracies in returns and complained to the Assembly of 1747; nor had ministers been calling for the £30. Another Act[27] reinforced the former and laid it upon synods to inspect the registers annually. It was becoming apparent too that some change would have to be made in the Act of Parliament if the scheme were to be surely based. Although Webster and Wallace had been overruled, they had been right when they wished the older ministers joining the fund to bear more of the burden if their widows were to have the same benefits as the widows of men who would pay premiums for a considerable number of years. The trustees prepared a representation for the Assembly of 1748.[28] The number of benefices and university appointments, totalling 1,013 was less by 26 than had been thought and the number of widows at 364 would be more by 43 than had been assumed. The stock would become stationary at £47,633 and then diminish. And £47,633 would be short by £10,000 of the sum required by 1771 if the capital were to rise to £63,860 by the time the greatest burden would fall on it. The representation was based on *Calculations with Principles and Data*, a careful analysis of the situation, probably by Webster, with the help of Halley's Tables, based on information from the city of Breslau. He had the help of George Drummond, the Lord Provost of Edinburgh, the Rev Matthew Stewart, Professor of Mathematics and Mr Alexander Chalmers, accountant, in the checking of the figures.[29] The Assembly agreed that changes were necessary and authority was given for another approach to Parliament. The trustees prepared a Memorial for the King in Parliament setting forth the changes desired, and the changes were given effect to in Act 22 Geo. II cap 21 amending 17 Geo. II cap II.[30]

The significant changes were as follows. If a minister should die before having paid a sum equal to three years' annuities corresponding to his annual rate, the allowance to his widow or children was to be reduced by the balance due, the widow receiving only one half annuity due until the balance was made up. The permitted capital, in addition to the £30 lent to each minister (amounting in all to approximately £30,000), was raised from £35,000 to £50,000. After payments of expenses the first charge on the income would be for the raising of this capital; from 1749 to 1752, £3,000; from 1753 to 1756, £2,000; from 1757 to 1763, £1,000; from 1764 to 1770, £400 and thereafter £200 per annum, until the sum of £50,000 be made up. In each year, after these deductions from the income, the annuities were to be made to widows in half-yearly instalments on 15th May and 11th November (old style—26th May and 22nd November, new style)[31] and stock to the children entitled. Should there be deficiency, the children's benefits and then the widows' would be reduced proportionately, the reduction being made good out of surpluses in subsequent years. If there should be further surplus in any year, after payment of expenses, capital increase, payment of annuities and stock to children and prior deficiencies, it would be added to capital. After the capital reached the required maximum, surpluses would be divided among widows and children in due proportion.

The trustees were authorised to raise the rate of interest to 5% on the £30 loans. Authority was given to the Lords of Session to issue general letters of horning at the collector's instance against ministers not paying rates, interest etc. The rate of payment was to be chosen on or before 26th January (new style) after the minister has had the right to stipend for one half-year (one year and a half if he lives in the Western or Northern Isles) or after a professor has held office for four months. (The trustee's year ran from 22nd November to 22nd November. Returns from presbyteries were due by 13th February, the date on which rates and marriage tax should be paid. The trustees considered the lists in March and arrangements for disposal of moneys in May. Annuities were paid on 26th May and 22nd November.)

One other change is interesting. The meetings of the trustees had been held in the Old Kirk Aisle in St Giles' building, a most uncomfortable and unsuitable place. In January 1745 they received some money from the Decima Fund of the Synod of Lothian and decided to build their own offices which they would then rent to the collector and clerk. The trustee's hall was duly ready by 1748, at Scot's Close in Edinburgh, and the Act authorised its use for meetings, four times a year and as required.

This Amending Act received the Royal Assent on 26th May 1749 and the Moderator of Assembly was authorised[32] to express thanks to the Chancellor, Speaker and Principal Secretaries of State for their help.

The need for the changes, comparatively minor as they were, arose from the fact that it had been assumed that the average payment would be £4 0s. 5d., the average annuity £15 6s. 4d. and the average stock to children £153 5s. In fact the average payment was £5 5s., the average annuity about £20 and payment to children £200.

From 1748 the actuality corresponded remarkably well to the calculated figures.[33] It was expected that 30 ministers and professors would die annually; there would be 20 new widows and six new families to be cared for each year.

Ministers and Professors

		Deaths	*(Calculated figure in brackets)*
5th April	1757	383	(390)
11th November	1759	468	(468)
	1762	537	(540)
22nd November	1764	615	(620)
22nd November	1777	981	(1,010)

New Widows

	1762	358	(360)
22nd November	1764	411	(413)
22nd November	1777	645	(673)

New Families

	1762	107	(108)
22nd November	1764	122	(124)
22nd November	1777	188	(202)

Number of Widows on Fund

5th April	1757	171	(177)
	1762	224	(229)
22nd November	1764	241	(250)?
22nd November	1777	305	(307)

The Average Annuity varied between £19 12s. and £20 18s. (£20)

The Average Rate was between £5 and £5 5s. (£5 5s.)

Free capital		£	£
	1748	18,290	(18,620)
	1756	42,888	(43,333)
	1759	49,128	(49,261)
	1761	52,122	(52,660)
	1764	57,468	(57,049)
	1765	58,347	(58,348)
	1778	75,088	(71,560)

(It appears that the calculated figure is as at Whitsunday and the actual figure as at Martinmas of the previous year.)

In 1757, the General Assembly, after hearing the Report of the Widows' Fund, passed an Act[34] instructing presbytery registers to be kept with the information about each parish under the heading of the parish and also authorising an abstract of the two Acts relative to the fund and the necessary forms and returns to be prepared and circulated to presbyteries and universities. Spare paper was to be bound up with the volume so that any new instructions might be entered in. The volume was ready by 1759.[35]

In 1771, Richard Price, Unitarian minister and pioneer actuary, published his Observations on Revisionary Payments and in the first editions expressed doubt about the soundness of the fund, because the premium payments were so low. Webster immediately wrote to him[36] and so persuaded him that in the third and subsequent editions he amended his judgement—"That part of the Second edition Chp. II which treats of the Scottish Establishment has now been new composed and carefully accommodated to the more accurate

information concerning it with which I have been favoured."
He also congratulated Webster, "the ingenious Doctor
Webster . . . the founder of this scheme."[37]

The importance of the fund in relationship to other
widows' funds and life insurance in general has, I believe,
not been sufficiently appreciated.

This is not the place even to summarise the history of life
insurance. Suffice it to say that early schemes were rather in
the nature of a gamble or were built on unsound principles.
Most, like that approved by the Assembly of 1742 against
the will of Webster and Wallace, were on the assessment
principle, the premiums of each year being distributed as
payments in that year. To work well this needs an attained
stationary membership and an ever-increasing membership
only puts off the day of reckoning. Only the Amicable
Society, founded in 1705, survived the South Sea Bubble of
1720 and it provided for a reserve although otherwise its
arrangements were largely on a variation of the assessment
principle.[38] The Scottish Ministers' Widows' Fund of 1744
was the first to operate on the maximum principle, capital
being gradually accumulated to such an extent that interest
and contributions would suffice to pay the maximum amount
of annuities and expenses likely to arise. It was of course a
compulsory scheme with a fairly stationary membership and
established by law. There was a life contingency dependent
on a fixed annual rate, chosen in advance. The benefits were
known in advance and provision was made for division of
any money surplus to requirements—the basis of the bonus
idea. There was no restriction on occupation if a minister be
deprived or resign, nor on place of residence.

The old Equitable Company of London was founded on
sound principles in 1762, but in the previous year the
first policy was issued by "The Corporation for the Relief of
poor and distressed Presbyterian Ministers, and of poor and
distressed Widows and Children of Presbyterian Ministers"
(22nd May 1761), in Philadelphia, Pennsylvania.[39] This
widows' and orphans' scheme led to the real beginning
of life insurance in America and when the Rev Francis
Alison, the minister of the First Presbyterian Church in
Philadelphia and the moving spirit in the Corporation,

applied for a charter, he used the words "in imitation of the laudable example of the Church of Scotland." The American Society was modelled very closely on the Scottish fund, and its historian acknowledges the fact very clearly.

Webster, in 1773, suggested alterations in the scheme and this resulted in a new Act, 19 Geo. III cap. 20, 1778, which repealed the first two Acts and was to remain normative, as amended by Acts in 1814 and 1890, until 1923. The 1778 Act made comparatively few changes but three were important. New entrants over 40 years of age if married or widowers with children, would pay an entry tax of two and a half annual rates. There were to be no more £30 loans to contributors and the existing ones were to be repaid with 4% interest. And the capital, including the loans, was to be raised to £100,000 as a maximum. When the total capital should reach £97,000, the trustees, after consulting contributors through universities and presbyteries, were to prepare a plan as to the disposal of surpluses. By 1798, the trustees were able to report that the £100,000 figure had been reached in the previous November.

References

˙This chapter is reproduced, with kind permission, from the Records of the Scottish Church History Society, vol XVII, pp 233-248, with some amendments.

[*References of the form "SRO: CH9/7/12" refer to the catalogue of documents held on behalf of the Scheme by the Scottish Record Office.*]

  1 cf. Cunningham: *Church History* II, p 319n. Crieff Kirk Session Minutes, 9th October 1709: "Mrs Strachan, the minister of Weems relict 12s."
  2 *Fasti Ecclesiae Scoticanae* IV, p 835, 1869 edition: "Jean Fleming relict of Mr James Smith minister of Eddleston iii c merks; Christian Gladstains, relict of Pat Weems iii c merks; Elspeth Petrey, relict of Mr James Chalmers ii c merks; and to the relict of Mr Will. Thomson, m. of Traquhair ii c merks."
  3 The papers are in the possession of the Ministers' Widows' Fund

and kept at the Scottish Record Office.

4 *Acts Gen. Ass.,* session V, 19th May, Church Law Society, 1843, p 520.

5 *Acts Gen. Ass.,* IV, 1723, p 564.

6 *Acts Gen. Ass.,* IV, 1735, p 631.

7 *An Account of the Rise of Nature of the Fund,* 1759, p 1.

8 N Morren: *Annals of the General Assembly of the Church of Scotland 1739-52,* 1838, p 28.

9 *Fasti Ecclesiae Scoticanae,* p 60.

10 Alexander Carlyle: *Autobiography,* 1860, pp 239ff. Jupiter Carlyle did not like Webster; cf. also Morren: *Annals 1752-66,* 1840, p 375.

11 Henry R Sefton: *An Early Moderate,* Scottish Church History Society XVI, p 11.

12 SRO: CH9/17/11: David Deuchar, in an inaugural address to the Actuarial Society of Edinburgh for the Session 1894-95 (*Proceedings of the Society* III, p 208f), made an interesting reconstruction of the probable calculations from a later point of view.

13 The Moderator had been asked by the Committee of Overtures to raise the matter of "renewing certain Schemes ... " in the morning of 14th May and a remit had been given to the Committee.

14 Webster: *Calculations with the principles and data on which they are instituted ... ,* Edinburgh, 1748.

15 cf. *Reasons in support ...* (1742): "But still this would involve the Church in the management of no small stock and many secular affairs not agreeable to her character ... inconveniency of lending money, purchasing land, uplifting annual rents, law suits, etc."

16 Morren: *Annals, 1739-52,* p 36.

17 Webster: *Calculations with the principles and data on which they are instituted,* Edinburgh, 1749.

18 SRO: CH9/17/2/1.

19 SRO: CH9/12/12. Maclaurin's name and support must have been of help to the commissioners in London.

20 SRO: CH9/17/23.

21 *Acts Gen. Ass.,* IV, 1744, p 674.

22 For Wallace, cf. Henry R Sefton: *An Early Moderate,* SCHS XVI, p 1; also Morren: *Annals 1739-52,* p 66.

23 cf. James G Kyd (ed): *Scottish Population Statistics,* SHS 1952.

24 Morren: *Annals, 1739-52,* p 66.

25 cf. SRO: CH9/17/23, Letter to *Edinburgh Courant.*

26 *Acts Gen. Ass.,* IV, 1745, p 680.

27 *Acts Gen. Ass.,* IV, 1747, p 693.

28 SRO: CH9/17/35: *The Representation of the Trustees ... to the General Assembly ...,* 1748.
29 *Fasti* I, p 151, 1915 edition: *Calculations with the principles and data ...,* 1748. He may also have had the help of Alexander Bryce, minister of Kirknewton and a man of scientific attainment.
30 *An Act for explaining and amending an Act*: reprinted Edinburgh, 1756.
31 Until recently, because of the eleven days difference when the new Calendar was introduced in 1753, the annuities from the pre-Union Church of Scotland section of the Fund, were payable on 26th May and 22th November, instead of at Whit Sunday and Martinmas, and the annual rate before 13th February instead of Candlemas.
32 Morren: *Annals, 1739-52*, p 157.
33 Morren: *Annals, 1752-66*, pp 132, 200, 261 and 309: Arnot: *History of Edinburgh*, 1788, p 544.
34 *Acts Gen. Ass.,* IV, 1757, p 728.
35 *An Account of the Rise and Nature of the Fund*, 1759.
36 *Letter, Rev Alex. Webster of Edinburgh to Rev Dr Price of London*, printed in Edinburgh, 1771; cf. Alexander Mackie: *Facile Princeps*, 1956, p 118.
37 William Morgan, Price's nephew and actuary to the Equitable of London also praised the Scots fund in the 7th Edition of *Observations on Revisionary Payments*, London, 1812.
38 The Amicable was amalgamated to the Norwich Union in 1864.
39 Alexander Mackie: *Facile Princeps*, 1956, p 109. This history of the beginning of life insurance in America, and particularly the Presbyterian Ministers' Fund, contains an excellent survey of the early Scottish Fund, pp 108-119.

CHAPTER 2

Early Actuarial Work
in Eighteenth-Century Scotland*

The Late James Bremner Dow MA FFA

I must begin with an apology. Ideally, a paper submitted to a sessional meeting of the Faculty should both throw light on some point of actuarial theory and show how that theory can be applied to solve some practical problem. This paper makes not the slightest attempt to do either of these things. It must be regarded as a piece of sheer escapism, whose existence can be justified—if, indeed, it can be justified at all—only by the possibility that others besides myself may find it interesting to discover how, before our Faculty or even our science existed, men approached some of the problems with which we are still concerned, and to find that at least the beginnings of actuarial thought in Scotland go back considerably farther in time than perhaps we had supposed. I should add that this paper is not so comprehensive as its title might suggest, since it deals only with the work done by two men, Robert Wallace and Alexander Webster on widows' funds and population statistics, and by a third, Colin Maclaurin, on a widows' fund. Even within these limits I am sure that much remains to be discovered by enquirers more skilled or more pertinacious than I am.

In his *History of the Faculty*,[1] A R Davidson wrote:

"The actuarial profession arose in Scotland, as elsewhere, from the requirements of the life offices."

and went on to show how the establishment of the first life assurance companies in Scotland in the early decades of the nineteenth century and the resulting demand for actuarial skills led to the foundation of the Faculty in 1856. He also pointed out, however, that, more than a century earlier, there were organisations in Scotland in need of the advice an actuary can give and cited as an example the "Church of Scotland Ministers' and Scottish University Professors' Widows' Fund" which was established in 1743 and which, he added, "is still in robust and healthy existence."

It is strange that a fund of actuarial character with a continuous history extending over two and a quarter centuries should have received as little attention in our professional writing as this fund has. There is an outline of its early story in an address given by David Deuchar to the Actuarial Society of Edinburgh in 1984,[2] but only a few brief passing references to it in our Transactions. Indeed, the fund has received more attention abroad than it has in this country, particularly from Alexander Mackie in his book *Facile Princeps*,[3] which is the history of the oldest American life assurance company, the Presbyterian Ministers' Fund. This company had its beginnings in a corporation which was set up in 1761 "in imitation of the laudable example of the Church of Scotland" for the relief of ministers and their widows. Mackie pays generous tribute to the pioneer work of the Church of Scotland, to the soundness of the principles on which the fund is based, and to the value of its example, an example also followed initially by the first Scottish life assurance company to be established, as the name Scottish Widows' Fund suggests. It is at these principles and at the men who evolved them that, I suggest, we might first look briefly.

Credit for founding the Church of Scotland fund is generally given to Dr Alexander Webster who was an eminent clergyman and a prominent figure in the Edinburgh of his day. Certainly he played a leading and, indeed, a vital part in setting it up, was the driving force behind its organisation and watched over its fortunes tirelessly from its inception until his death in 1784, but, in fact, the records of the fund suggest that the calculations on which the scheme was based, and which could be described as actuarial, were largely the work of another clergyman, Dr Robert Wallace and of Colin

Maclaurin the mathematician, who have therefore a good claim to be, if not the first Scottish Actuaries, at least the first Scotsmen to think actuarially. As, in addition, Wallace thought and wrote a great deal on demographic questions—indeed, in the *Dictionary of National Biography* he is described as a "writer on population"—and as Webster also carried out the first census of Scotland in or about the year 1755 it seems that the lives and work of these men merit some reference in our Transactions.

Robert Wallace was born in 1697 at Kincardine "in the stewartry of Menteith and the county of Perth" where his father was parish minister. After attending the grammar school at Stirling the young Robert went in 1711 to Edinburgh University where his course of study included classes in language, logic, metaphysics, mathematics, physics, ethics, and theology. He was evidently both an able and popular student, and, in 1717, with some others he set up a debating society called the Rankenian Club, the name being that of the proprietor of the tavern where the club's meetings were held. In this, as in most student societies, papers were read and discussed and the affairs of the world put to rights, but, despite its convivial environment, the club's aims were serious. Members entered into correspondence with Bishop Berkeley, who was so impressed with their grasp of his philosophical ideas that he invited them to go to Bermuda to staff the college he was planning to found there. Fortunately they declined the invitation and remained in Scotland, to whose national and literary life many of them made notable contributions.

As a student Wallace showed particular aptitude for mathematics and, indeed, in the session of 1720–21, during the illness of the professor of mathematics, Dr James Gregory, Wallace conducted the mathematics classes with complete acceptance. He had decided, however, to enter the Church, was licensed in 1722 and in the following year was appointed to his first charge in Moffat. Here he remained until 1733 when he returned to Edinburgh to become minister of New Greyfriars Church. In 1735 he was one of the group which, under the leadership of Colin Maclaurin, who had succeeded Gregory as professor of mathematics at

Edinburgh, founded the Philosophical Society. Wallace later made some important contributions to the proceedings of this society which, in 1783, was reconstituted and enlarged in scope to become the Royal Society of Edinburgh.

After the civil disturbance of 1736 which came to be known as the Porteous Riots, Wallace fell into disfavour with the authorities because, along with some other ministers of the Church of Scotland, he refused to read from his pulpit each month a government proclamation threatening the severest penalties to anyone giving aid or comfort to the rioters, but after the fall of Walpole's government in 1742, his position was reversed and he became one of the new government's chief advisers on ecclesiastical appointments in Scotland. This was a post of considerable importance, because the system of patronage still prevailed and something like one third of the charges in Scotland were in the grant of the crown. Prior to this, in 1739, he had been appointed minister of the Edinburgh charge of New North, where he remained until his death in 1771, and it was soon after taking up this charge that his connection with the widows' fund and with Alexander Webster began.

At this time Webster was minister of the Tolbooth Church in Edinburgh which worshipped in what was then a rather ramshackle corner of the Kirk of St Giles, and took its name from the adjoining Tolbooth prison. It may be remembered as the setting for a dramatic incident in an early chapter of Sir Walter Scott's *Heart of Midlothian* when one of the condemned smugglers escapes from his guards during his last church service before execution. Webster, who was born in 1707, was the son of a former minister of the Tolbooth, had been educated at the High School and University of Edinburgh where, like Wallace, he had shown more than a little mathematical ability, and, before coming to the Tolbooth in 1737, had been for four years minister of the ancient burgh of Culross in Fife. Indeed, for Webster, 1737 was something of an *annus mirabilis*, because soon after he came to Edinburgh he married a Miss Mary Erskine, a young lady of good family and considerable fortune. This story is told that Webster was asked by a very bashful friend to approach Miss Erskine and put to her a proposal of marriage on the friend's behalf. The young minister expended his eloquence on the lady in vain until finally she interrupted with the remark, "You would come better speed, Sandy, if you spoke for yoursel'." As one narrator rather coyly puts it, "the hint was too obvious to be overlooked and its promise too agreeable to be neglected." Sandy did speak for himsel' and succeeded. It would only be a slight exaggeration to say that they lived happily ever after.

From 1698 onwards the Church of Scotland had made several attempts to organise financial provision for the widows and orphans of its ministers. Various schemes, mostly of a voluntary or charitable nature, had been put forward and tried but all had failed through inadequate support or imperfect organisation. In 1741 the need for action was again recognised and a group of Edinburgh ministers, which included Wallace and Webster, applied themselves to the problem. Clearly Webster was the driving force. He was a man of great energy and initiative and although he does not appear to have had any official status or authority, he wrote to all the presbyteries in Scotland asking them to produce from their records information about the number of their members dying, the numbers leaving widows with and without children, the numbers of widows still alive and unmarried and so on, the statistics to cover the period from March 1722 to March 1742. To those who know the ways of presbyteries the fact that full or nearly full replies were received to these apparently unofficial enquiries will sufficiently attest the force of Webster's personality.

Meanwhile Wallace was applying himself to consider the theoretical basis of a widows' fund and set out his ideas in a manuscript which has been preserved in the records of the fund and which may well be one of the earliest actuarial documents in the world. It is almost certainly the first attempt to organise scientifically a widows' fund on an annual premium basis and so is of historic interest to actuaries. To anyone, whether actuary or not, it is a fascinating illustration of how a man of intelligent mind, with no resources but his own intelligence, can attack a completely new and strange problem and arrive at eminently sensible conclusions. The manuscript, which is undated but seems to have been written in 1741 or 1742, is reproduced in full in Appendix 1, and although it would take too long to go through it in detail, I would like to draw your attention to one or two points in it:

(i)   The argument in paragraph 3, which leads him to conclude that "every widow may have the quadruple of what her husband pays in and therefore a triple cannot be too much." This is an example of the intuitive argument by which actuaries still put a rough check on their formal calculations, and it is also probably the first recorded case in actuarial history of a contingency margin in a premium. In fact, the ratio of annuity to contribution finally adopted was just under four.

(ii) The number of what we now regard as the classical problems of widows' funds which Wallace appreciated, e.g. health risk, selective force of marriage, husband older than wife, entrants at old ages, etc.

(iii) The simple and practical draft rules he proposes, many of which with minor alterations could appear in the constitution of a modern fund.

As the return from the presbyteries came in, Wallace set to work and made numerous calculations, some based on partial, others on complete or nearly complete statistics. He clearly realised that he was dealing with as close an approximation to the stationary population of actuarial theory as is likely to be achieved in real life, since the number of parishes, and hence of ministers, in Scotland was at this time virtually constant and most men entered the ministry at age 26 or thereby. Accordingly he used Halley's Breslau table to make a population estimate assuming an annual entry to the ministry of 30 men aged 26, and drew up a table of the numbers surviving to each year of age. By carrying the calculation up to age 84, the limiting age of Halley's table, he found that the total population on his assumptions would be 927, compared with the population of 970 which the 26 annual entrants to the Church appeared to support in real life.

If the returns were really completed up to March 1742

then subsequent progress was incredibly rapid. A special meeting of the General Assembly was called on 8th May 1742 "for receiving any schemes or proposals that may be offered for raising a fund for the widows of Ministers", at which meeting "any member of this Assembly or minister of this church may be heard." This was probably done so that Webster, who was not a member of the Assembly that year, could present the plan which Wallace and he had devised. It was a sophisticated one, offering a choice of four grades of contributions ranging from $2\frac{1}{2}$ guineas to $6\frac{1}{4}$ guineas with proportional widows' annuities ranging from £10 per annum to £25 per annum. In addition, a capital sum of "stock" equal to ten times the annuity was to be payable to the children of those members who left no widow. There was also a provision that both annuities and capital sums would be reduced to the dependants of members who died in the early years of membership—probably the earliest recorded example of an initial debt.

The Assembly rejected this plan, "it being alledged . . . that it would not sufficiently relieve the Indigent and Necessitous and being apprehensive of some Difficulties in managing a capital. . . ."[4] Instead, it put forward for consideration by presbyteries an alternative plan under which all widows would receive an annuity of £20 and there would be no benefit for children. Members would be assessed yearly an amount sufficient to meet the annuities arising that year, the maximum assessment to be £4. Should that prove insufficient the deficit would be met by levy on the previous year's entrants to the ministry up to a maximum of £20, and, if more should still be needed, ministers with the highest stipends would be called on to pay more than £4.

The impracticability of the Assembly's plan becomes immediately clear when we consider the level of stipends in 1742. The minimum stipend for ministers for the Church of Scotland had been fixed in 1633 at £45 per annum and an enquiry to be made in 1749 would show that some 200 ministers were even then receiving this minimum stipend or less. The payments which would eventually fall on new entrants might therefore be as much as half their first year's stipend and were clearly too high to be contemplated, particularly as Wallace's calculations showed that the £4 limit would probably be passed in 11 or 12 years and the £20 maximum would be in force from about the 16th year onwards.

Quite rightly, the presbyteries were strongly critical of this scheme and, faced with objections, the Commission of Assembly which met in November 1742 took the familiar course of appointing a large committee of both ministers and laymen including Wallace and Webster. With uncharacteristic but commendable speed this committee sent a revised plan to the presbyteries in January 1743, inviting them to comment on it before March or, at latest, before the meeting of Assembly in May. This timetable was adhered to and the *Scots Magazine* for May 1743, in reporting the proceedings of the Assembly, was able to say:

> "The Scheme for providing an annuity to the widows and a stock to the children of ministers . . . was considered in a committee of the whole house and with some amendments transmitted to the Assembly: who, after reasoning, approved of them and resolved to apply for an act."

Appropriately, Wallace was Moderator of this Assembly and he and another Edinburgh minister, the Rev George Wishart, were appointed commissioners to arrange for the necessary bill to be prepared and presented to parliament.

The scheme now approved was the same as the one which the Assembly had rejected the previous year, with two modifications to meet the objections which had then been raised:

(i)   Full benefits were to be payable from the beginning of membership.

(ii) To reduce the problems of investment each member was required to take a loan of £30 from the fund at 4% interest. These loans were to be taken up as money became available, an order of presbyteries being prescribed for this purpose. These loans would eventually total almost £30,000, and the fund was to be allowed to accumulate a further £35,000 of assets, after which any excess would be used to pay additional benefits to the children of members.

The scheme was to be optional for existing ministers but compulsory for future entrants to the ministry. The principals and professors of the Scottish universities, many of whom were at this time ministers of the Church of Scotland, anyway, were to be eligible for membership if the individual universities chose to join, and in the event all did.

For this scheme, too, Wallace made very extensive calculations. He made various assumptions about the proportions of entrants who would select the different levels of benefit and, with a meticulous care which we can admire to a point just short of imitation, calculated, using Halley's tables, the expected number of widows in each grade correct to six places of decimals. Using the "guess" in his original memorandum that the widow's annuity might be about quadruple the annual contribution, he traced the probable future progress of the fund up to the time when the maximum number of widows would be entitled to benefit. After many pages of laborious but orderly arithmetic he concluded that a tax of $2\frac{1}{2}$ guineas for the lowest class with other classes in proportion would, as he put it, "answer all exigencies" and this was the basis adopted.

After the plan had been approved by the Assembly in May 1743, progress seems to have been uninterrupted. In July a circular was sent out signed by Wallace as Moderator detailing the provisions of the scheme and commending it to the Church. There is no record of any objections. A draft bill was prepared with the help of some eminent Scottish lawyers and, after the Commission of Assembly at its November meeting had approved it, Wallace and Wishart with the good wishes of their brethren left for London where they arrived on 3rd December. (Perhaps we might pause for a moment to remind ourselves what that journey then involved. Until 1760 only one stage-coach regularly left Edinburgh for London each week. Depending on the weather and the condition of the roads which in winter were frequently impassable, the journey took anything up to fourteen days and passengers usually made their wills before setting out.)

The timing of the visit could hardly have been more unfortunate. In court and government circles much anxiety already existed about the possibility of rebellion in Scotland— a possibility which was to become reality in 1745. In 1742 Walpole's government had fallen in discredit and the prestige of Parliament, as well as its ability to deal effectively with the problems of the nation, was suspect. Altogether the chance that Parliament would find time or would be inclined to consider, let alone approve, a purely Scottish bill aimed at setting up a strange new scheme to help the widows of Scottish clergymen seemed less than minimal. Private correspondence shows that many leading figures in public life in Scotland took this view. On the other hand Wallace, as we have seen, was the government's adviser on ecclesiastical matters in Scotland and in this capacity had served them quietly and well, so that he had some claim to official goodwill. Moreover, though he was known to his friends as "the philosopher" there seems to have been nothing abstract or impractical about his thinking or his actions. Wishart and he met all the Scottish members of Parliament and sought the support of everyone who might ease the passage of the bill. In all this they were advised, though not noticeably assisted, by a steady stream of letters from their committee in Edinburgh, to few of which they seem to have replied, and then only to say that the committee's advice had been overtaken by events and that they had done something quite different from what they had been told to do. The committee's letters, which show a steadily mounting sense of frustrated authority, have been preserved among Wallace's papers, and on the folder containing them he has written the pleasantly wry comment:

> "Messrs Wallace and Wishart served the church with fidelity and care, they succeeded and they had the thanks of the General Assembly and all good men. But when they were at London several peevish and unwise orders were sent them and they learned by experience how difficult it was to be directed and advised by a Committee at Edinburgh."

The bill went through all its parliamentary stages in the Commons and the Lords and received the royal assent on 3rd March 1744. Its full title was "An Act for raising and Establishing a Fund for a Provision for the Widows and Children of the Ministers of the Church of Scotland, and of the Heads, Principals, and Masters of the Universities of St Andrews, Glasgow, and Edinburgh" (17 George II, cap. 2). King's and Marischal Colleges, Aberdeen, joined later. The effective starting date of the Fund was fixed as 25th March 1744, and we may reflect a little sadly that these figures must be well below the par for a similar legislative course today. At the General Assembly in May, Wallace and Wishart were thanked for their "faithfulness and diligence in soliciting the obtaining of the Act." Webster also received the thanks of the Assembly "for the extraordinary pains and trouble taken by him in the rise and progress of the scheme."

At this point, with the Act on the statute book and the Fund in being, it is convenient to look at the part played in its founding by Colin Maclaurin, who had been professor of mathematics at Edinburgh University since 1725.

To actuaries of my generation Maclaurin is known as the co-author with Euler of a formula of numerical integration, although in fact this was probably among the least of his achievements. He was born in 1698, the son of an Argyllshire minister who, after the early deaths of his parents, was brought up by his uncle who was also a minister in Argyll. He showed early and outstanding promise as a mathematician and at the age of 15, when graduating from Glasgow University, he delivered and defended a public dissertation on the power of gravity in which he showed his grasp of the then revolutionary principles of Newtonian physics. After some years of quiet study at his uncle's manse he was appointed professor of mathematics at Aberdeen shortly after his nineteenth birthday. His first book dealing with some geometrical problems quickly followed and earned him the fellowship of the Royal Society at the almost indecently early age of 21. During a visit to London he made the acquaintance of Sir Isaac Newton, who formed the highest opinion of the young man's ability. In 1725, when an appointment to the Edinburgh chair of mathematics was made necessary by the incapacity of its holder, Newton pressed Maclaurin's claims on the Corporation with whom the decision lay and even offered, if the payment of two salaries created any financial problem, to pay part of Maclaurin's salary himself.

By this time Maclaurin had established himself as a mathematician and thinker of international reputation, second in Britain only to Newton. He was, moreover, a brilliant and popular teacher and his lectures made mathematics one of the fashionable subjects of study in the Edinburgh of the 1730s. He was also much in demand as a consultant and advised on such diverse questions as the preparation of new maps of northern Scotland, exploring for the long-sought North West passage, dredging the estuary of the River Clyde, and, with the Customs and Excise as client, the best method of estimating the volume of liquid in a container. His last remit was probably his strangest. In September 1745 he was one of a small group of Edinburgh citizens who pressed on a reluctant Lord Provost the need to do something to defend the city against the advancing Jacobite army. Maclaurin's particular task was to repair the fortifications of the castle and the walls of the city. With such helpers as he could muster, including his pupil, the architect-to-be Robert Adam, he toiled prodigiously in the few days before the rebel forces reached the city; but, unfortunately, his work was never tested, as the government troops under Sir John Cope, who were to man the defences, were still on their way from Aberdeen when Prince Charles and his men entered the city.

As a result of these exertions and of subsequent hardships while avoiding capture by the Jacobite forces, Maclaurin contracted an illness from which he died in June 1746 at the age of 48, a sad loss to science and to Scotland. Until a few hours before his death he was working on a book entitled *An Account of the Philosophical Ideas of Sir Isaac Newton*, which was published posthumously in 1748. It contains a biographical note based on a memorial lecture delivered by Alexander Monro, who was Dean of the Faculty of Medicine at Edinburgh University and a close friend of Maclaurin. This memoir contains the following passage:

". . . but what must have given him a higher satisfaction than anything else of this kind . . . was the calculations he made relative to that wise and humane provision which is now established by law for the children and widows of the Scotch clergy and of the professors in the universities . . . In contriving and adjusting the scheme Mr Maclaurin had bestowed great labour; and the gentlemen who were appointed to solicit the affair at London own that the authority of his name was of great use to them for removing any doubts that were moved concerning the sufficiency of the proposed fund or the due proportion of the sums and annuities."

Coming from such a source, these words must carry great weight. Indeed, it is difficult to believe that Maclaurin would not be involved, or at least asked for advice. Wallace and he were close friends, and, if you are lucky enough to count one of the great mathematicians of Europe among your friends, you will naturally consult him when you are involved in new and strange calculations. In the records of the fund, however, the only signs of MacLaurin's involvement are two letters and a sheet of tables marked "Tables for the Widows' Scheme 1743." On the outside of the sheet of tables there is a note in Wallace's writing, "I think they were made by Mr Colin Maclaurin." The headings of the tables and the letters are reproduced in Appendices II, IV and V, along with a third letter which is in the library of Edinburgh University and which helps to explain the other two (Appendix III). It will be seen that the letters are dated after the scheme had been approved by the Assembly and seem to have been written by someone who had been asked to examine and comment on the scheme and not by one who had any claim to be its author. No doubt, in addition to any informal discussions which Maclaurin may have had with Wallace, he would be asked by the university authorities to report on the soundness of the plan before they committed the university to join. The letter of 3rd June is almost an actuarial certificate, bearing the authority of Maclaurin's name, which Wallace and Wishart would certainly use when they were lobbying for the bill in London, as Maclaurin's biographer suggests. Indeed, the letter may have been requested for this purpose.

Once the fund was in being, Wallace's interest in it seems to have diminished. He was one of the trustees who attended meetings, served on committees and occasionally acted as chairman, but there is no evidence in the trustees' minutes that he acted in any sense as a leader. He had, of course, many other interests. In 1753 he published a book with the title *A Dissertation on the Number of Mankind in Ancient and Modern Times*, the substance of which had earlier appeared as a paper to the Philosophical Society. It is an impressive display of erudition in which many of the references in ancient literature to the numbers of peoples or armies are used to make estimates of population and in which he sharply disagrees with the arguments and conclusions of a chapter in David Hume's book *Political Discourses*. For all Wallace's learning, however, we may today doubt whether, for example, the statements of a victorious general regarding the number of the enemy whom he killed or took prisoner make a firm basis for estimating the population of the defeated nation, although we may have to admit there is no better available.

In 1761 Wallace published another and more important work entitled *Various Prospects of Mankind, Nature and Providence* which so far anticipated the thesis later put forward by Malthus that Hazlitt[5] in more than one essay accused Malthus of borrowing all that was of substance in his book from Wallace.

In the fierce ecclesiastical controversies of his time Wallace seldom became publicly involved. He was widely respected both inside and outside the Church for his intellectual abilities, and his personal qualities brought him many friends and few enemies. One historian, Sir Henry Craik, has written of him:[6]

"It was, indeed, chiefly by his amazing versatility that he was characteristic of his time: and in the midst of all his various activities and speculations he found time for the delights of social intercourse, of which Edinburgh was then the choicest of centres, and left behind him, when he died in 1771, a memory of the most cultivated, the most ingenious, and the most courteous of companions."

To an audience in Edinburgh the manner of his death is perhaps of some interest. In the early part of the month of May 1771 he went for a walk in what was then the pleasant open country to the north of his hall. (The Actuaries' Hall, St Andrew's Square.) He was caught in a snowstorm, contracted a chill, and from the resulting complications died in July.

In contrast to Wallace, Webster's connection with the fund remained close and active. He was involved in all its activities from designing the clerk's record books to supervising the building of a hall where the trustees could meet. He was severely and publicly critical of the older ministers because they opted for the largest annuities, and of the younger ministers because they did not join the fund at all, and he was quick to see that this made Wallace's estimates of the fund's future progress too optimistic, particularly as it was soon apparent that there had been errors in the information supplied by the presbyteries which had resulted in the probable number of widows being underestimated. Out of a possible 962, only 827 had elected to join, which meant that the fund could not grow as quickly as the forecast required. Accordingly, in 1747 a committee was appointed which included besides Webster and Wallace and other clergymen, Lord Provost Drummond, Matthew Stewart, who had succeeded Maclaurin as professor of mathematics at Edinburgh, and Alexander Chalmers, chief accountant to the Customs and Excise in Scotland. To deal with the situation the committee put forward a proposal which, as they said, "had frequently been suggested to some of the Trustees by the late ingenious and accurate Mr Maclaurin" and which is referred to in the tables and letters of the Appendices: namely, that if a member die before the rates he has paid amount to three years' annuity, the widow's annuity will be reduced to half until the balance is made up. The committee's proposals were approved by the Assembly and an act of 1748 amended the fund accordingly. It also increased from £35,000 to £50,000 the amount which the free capital must reach before any additional benefits could be paid.

To support its proposals and to explain them to the members the committee published a memorandum with very extensive calculations showing the rise and progress of the fund and its probable future growth if the amendments were adopted. A similar memorandum with further calculations followed in 1759. These calculations were all based on Halley's Breslau table, average numbers of yearly entrants, average ages and so on, and as actuaries we can note with interest that their forecasts proved uncannily accurate. By 1758, for example, the fund amounted to £47,313:19:9 compared with a forecast of £47,401, and by 1765 to £58,347:17:8 compared with a forecast of £58,348:17:8. Could any computer-based estimate of future cash flow do better?

By 1748 Webster had become a well-known figure in the life of Edinburgh and indeed of Scotland. He was a very popular, though not apparently a very profound, preacher whose church was packed every Sunday, so that one Edinburgh citizen was heard to hope that it would be easier to get into the kingdom of Heaven than it was to get a seat in the Tolbooth Kirk. In 1753 he was elected Moderator of the General Assembly and about this time he was apparently asked by someone in authority to carry out a census of Scotland to discover how many fighting men the country could be expected to muster. No doubt in the official view the natural pugnacity of the Scots would be better employed in facing a foreign army than in assisting Charles Edward Stewart in a repetition of 1745. Again Webster approached this completely unfamiliar task in a characteristically practical and forthright way. Through the widows' fund he had, as he put it, "established a correspondence with many of the ministers of Scotland." This is possibly a polite eighteenth-century euphemism meaning that he had written them stern letters telling them to send in their statistical returns or pay their contributions to the fund more promptly, and that they had learned to do what he asked. He was also chairman of the Society for Propagating Christian Knowledge, a charitable organisation which helped to pay the costs of providing schools in rural parishes, particularly in the Highlands. He asked each minister to count the number of his parishioners, more than a hint being given to the members of the second group that if they did not co-operate, the grants for their schools might stop.

The results of this census, which is generally taken to relate to the year 1755, though some of the data may have been collected either earlier or later, have been analysed by the late Mr J G Kyd, our former President, and are published in the proceedings of the Scottish History Society (1952)[7] and so I shall not discuss them further here, except to say that Webster estimated the population of Scotland to be 1,265,380, of whom he thought one-fifth "may be reckoned effective men." According to Dr J C Dunlop this was only the third census taken anywhere in Europe since the fall of the Roman Empire, the previous ones being in Sweden 1749 and in Austria in 1754. It is certainly the only national estimate of population in Britain made prior to the first official census of 1801 on which any reliance can be placed.

Whatever the purpose of Webster's enquiry, his manuscript remained in the Advocates' Library and his results do not appear to have been published until Kyd's paper appeared in 1952, though the figures were examined by Dr Dunlop in 1921 when he arranged for a copy of them to be put in the National Library of Scotland. This seems to suggest that Webster was not allowed to use his results for the other purposes which he clearly saw they might serve. For example, he pointed out that a table he had constructed showing the population according to age "might serve several purposes particularly for calculating the probabilities of life and consequently for estimating the value of annuities in Scotland with more exactness than any Tables yet extant." From the same table he deduced that "the generality of People in Scotland live to a greater age than at London, and not to so great an age as at Breslau." I have found no evidence, however, that he brought his census information to the service of the widows' fund.

By the time he became Moderator in 1753 Webster had emerged as the accepted leader of the Evangelical party in the Church of Scotland. This party claimed to have inherited and to maintain the pure doctrine of the Convenanters in all its austerity, and had no sympathy for the more tolerant views of their opponents, the Moderates, to whom, incidentally, Wallace belonged. Between the two parties disagreements were frequent and bitter, and in the resultant debates Webster made many enemies. It is possible that his reputation has suffered somewhat because many contemporary references to him come from the writings of his ecclesiastical opponents.

From the long list of pleasures which the Evangelicals did not permit themselves, one notable omission was the consumption of claret, and in this respect also Webster was their acknowledged leader. That shrewd commentator on eighteenth century Scotland and Scotsmen, John Ramsay of Ochtertyre,[8] wrote:

> "It was hardly in the power of liquor to affect Dr Webster's understanding or his limbs."

And clearly, he wrote in envy and not in criticism. In support of Ramsay's statement we may note that Webster spent the evening of 17th August 1773 in the company of Dr Johnson and Boswell and emerged apparently unscathed, for Boswell reported:[9]

> "At supper we had Dr Alexander Webster, who, though not learned, had such a knowledge of mankind, such a fund of information and entertainment, so clear a head and such accommodating manners, that Dr Johnson found him a very agreeable companion."

A later historian,[10] after describing Webster as the most able businessman of the whole city who made the plans for the New Town, added that he:

> ". . . combined the clearest of heads with the most unctuous of spirits, was the life of the supper parties of Edinburgh any time between 1760 and 1780, could join over a magnum of claret on Monday with gentlemen of not too correct lives whom he had professionally consigned to

perdition on Sunday. He could pass with alacrity and sincerity from devout prayers by a bedside to a roystering reunion in Fortune's tavern and return home with his Bible under his arm and five bottles under his girdle."

Whether Webster actually "made the plans for the New Town" we may take leave to doubt, but he was a member of the Lord Provost's committee which did and he would certainly make his contribution. One cannot picture Webster in the role of sleeping partner.

Webster seems to have become recognised as something of an authority on widows' funds. In January 1768, for example, the United Incorporations of St Mary's Chapel sought his advice on how to set one up. This body, which is still in existence, was formed in 1475 by the union of various guilds of craftsmen in the city of Edinburgh such as masons, wrights, coopers, painters and others. Entrants were required to execute a test piece of work to the satisfaction of examiners before they were admitted to the privileges of membership which included payments to widows and dependants. These had been met by levying the members on an assessment basis, but Webster recommended a scheme which in many of its provisions followed closely the pattern of the Church's scheme but with one scale of contributions and benefits. This plan was put into operation in March 1768—again we may wistfully ask whether it would be done as quickly today—and it is still in healthy existence, though with a small membership.

The Church of Scotland widows' fund enters what may be called official actuarial history in 1771 when Richard Price, who was by then consultant to the Equitable Life Assurance Society and who is now remembered chiefly as the author of the Northampton Tables, published his book *Observations on Reversionary Payments*. In it he criticised the Church of Scotland scheme on the ground that the contributions were too low. Webster reacted immediately and on 4th October 1771 he wrote Price a letter of nearly 5000 words[11] in which, as he put it:

"I take the opportunity of acquainting you with some essential parts of the scheme of which I find you had no information and to explain others of which your information has been imperfect."

Price replied on 21st October—which in 1771 was certainly by return—and agreed that he had not fully understood the plan and promised to rewrite the offending passage in later editions. These, in fact, commended the soundness of the plan and paid tribute to the "great ability and faithful Zeal of the Rev Dr Webster, its founder and conductor." After Price's death further editions of the book were prepared by Price's nephew, William Morgan, and as it remained a standard actuarial textbook for nearly a century, the existence and reputation of the fund came to be widely known.

The fund's first connection with the Faculty came through W T Thomson, who valued it at November 1849 and again at November 1861. As we might expect, the reports on these valuations—copies of which are in our library—are models of their kind, lucid and comprehensive with all the arguments impressively supported by statistics. The valuation of 1849 was an interesting one as it covered the period of the Disruption of 1843 when many ministers left the Church of Scotland to found the Free Church. Some retained their rights under the fund and as the vacant parishes were filled by new entrants the membership and liabilities of the fund increased. The financial consequences to the fund were, however, safely overcome. Indeed, it is an interesting example of the long-term aspect of some actuarial affairs that the rates of contribution, which had been increased in 1814 from $2\frac{1}{2}$ to 3 guineas for the lowest grade with proportionate increases in the other grades, were still in force when the Churches reunited in 1929. At that date the basis of the fund was changed for future entrants, but there are still a few widows of ministers in the service of the Church of Scotland whose husbands were members of the fund before 1929.

In conclusion, I would like to record my thanks to those who have helped me, in particular to the Rev A Ian Dunlop, the present Chairman of the Trustees of the Church and Universities Widows' Fund, who is an authority on the fund's history and has been very generous in passing on his knowledge, and to the Rev H R Sefton and to Mrs Norah Smith who have kindly made available to me the results of their research into Wallace's theological and literary work.

I end as I began—with an apology for detaining you so long in the byways of two hundred years ago. I confess that I am under the spell of the curious magic of eighteenth-century Edinburgh which caused everything done in that time and place to be done well, whether it was setting up a widows' fund, establishing a medical school or building a new town. I confess too that I find it interesting and heartening to discover that, in this city, before any of the problems which concern the actuary had been scientifically approached, three men of such diverse character and abilities as Maclaurin, Wallace and Webster were addressing themselves to some of the more complicated actuarial operations with that mixture of theory and common sense which we flatter ourselves is still the mark of the good actuary today. I am very happy to find them among my professional ancestors.

References

*This chapter is reproduced, with kind permission, of the Council of the Faculty of Actuaries. It was originally delivered as a lecture to the Faculty of Actuaries on 16th October 1972, and was followed by a good discussion. The lecture and discussion are contained in the Transactions of the Faculty, vol 33, part 3.

1 A R Davidson: History of the Faculty of Actuaries in Scotland 1856-1956.

2 D Deuchar: "Notes on Widows' Funds" from Transactions of the Actuarial Society of Edinburgh, vol iii, p 61.

3 Alexander Mackie: *Facile Princeps*, ch VIII.

4 Quoted from a report issued in 1748 by the Committee appointed to review the progress of the fund. A copy of this report can be found among the records of the fund in the Scottish Record Office.

5 Examples are the essays entitled: "An examination of Mr Malthus's Essay" and "Queries relating to the Essay on Population."

6 Sir Henry Craik: *A Century of Scottish History*, vol 1.

7　J G Kyd, *Scottish Population Statistics*, Scottish History Society XLIII, 1952.
8　Allardyce (ed): *Scotland and Scotsmen in the Eighteenth Century from the Mss of John Ramsay of Ochtertyre.*
9　James Boswell: *Journal of a Tour to the Hebrides with Samuel Johnson LLD.*
10　H Graham: *The Social Life of Scotland in the Eighteenth Century.*
11　This correspondence was published by Murray and Cochrane. There is a copy in the National Library of Scotland.

Appendix I

Manuscript in Wallace's handwriting, undated, but probably written in 1741 *or* 1742.

Proposals for raising a fund for jointures to the widows of such gentlemen as have not lands, estates nor great sums of money but live by their business or yearly income which depends on their lives.

1.　It is proposed that a society be formed of the husbands, adventurers, the contributors to this fund.

2.　That every husband pay in yearly to this society what sum he thinks proper during his life & that his widow shall draw after his death a proportionable sum during her life.

This method is judged better than that a compleat sum be given in all at once because this proposal is principally intended for gentlemen who have not great sums of money but may be able to spare something out of their yearly income.

Besides it will be easier to settle a sum for the widow in this manner than if a great sum be given at once.

3.　It is experience alone & a nice calculation that must determine the proportional sum the widow is to have after the husband's death but a beginning may be made by allowing triple the sum the husband payed in during his life so if a husband payes yearly 10L the widow has 30L if he pay 30L she draws 90L during her life.

It is judged this proportion will not be too great considering that the husband has as good if not a better chance to be the survivor so the half or more than the half of the widows will want no jointure which alone makes the Society able to give double or near to double of what the husband pays (for by the exactest calculation the Society is not to be allowed to be very rich but to depend chiefly on their yearly incomes and not on the rents of lands or interests of money). But besides this as the ordinary time of marrying and consequently of entering into this society (as we shall see afterwards) is about 30 years of age and persons at 30 by the bills of mortality may be supposed to live about 28 years, this makes the common time that marryed persons live together about 28 years and 58 to be the common time when a woman is a widow. But persons at 58 years of age by the bills of mortality have an equal chance to live only 13 years which is not half the time that married persons live together. That is to say the Society has only half the number of widows to provide and this half only half the time of their husbands contributing yearly to the Society; that is every widow may have the quadruple of what the husband pays in and therefore a triple cannot be too much.

But the proportioning of this sum according to the exigencies of the Society must be left either to the Court of Directors or to the annual meeting of the whole contributors as shall be most expedient.

4.   Married persons are supposed to be much about an age or they may be supposed to have nearly an equall chance for living tho' the husband be somewhat elder because of the risk of bearing children.

It is proposed therefore that if the husband be not above 10 years older than his wife he be allowed to enter into this Society according to the above proposals.

5.   But if the husband be more than 10 years older than his wife besides the yearly sum he payes, for every year above 10 he must give a premium for his privellege of entering into the Society. This premium is to be payed all at once at entering into the Society or at the outmost at 3 terms. The Determination of this premium depends on a nice calculation. Thus suppose a man be 15 years older than his wife had

he been 5 years younger than he is he had been freed, to make all equal then he must pay 5 years advance, that is 50L of premium if he is to pay yearly 10L. But this will make too great a sum payable as a premium there must therefore be some abatement made by making it only a half or 3rd of this sum, but still it must be some proportional part of his yearly income.

6.   Tho' a man shall dy tomorrow after he enters into the Society his widow shall be entitled to her jointure and he shall be obliged to the first years payment provided a man enter into the society within a year of his marriage or the first constitution of the Society but no man must be allowed to enter upon his death bed or when it is visible that he is dying to prevent which it may be constituted that every man must not only come to transact this with the Directors but that the bargain shall not be finished till 3 months after the first proposal and the man be personally present.

7.   But if he do not enter within a year of his marriage or constitution of the Society besides all other regulations concerning him he must live a full year after he enters into the Society without which his widow shall not be entitled to her jointure.

8.   A man is to be allowed to enter into the Society any year of his life but if he dont enter within a year of his marriage or the constitution of the Society he must besides his yearly payments advance to the Society a sum equal to all his payments supposing he had entered into the Society within a year after his marriage. But because this sum will be too great & equivalent to a total excluding great numbers out of the Society it may be considered whether any abatement may be made of this and what these abatements shall be.

To show that the Society has the best chance by people entering into it soon and not long after their marriage suppose 2 couple enter into the Society the one couple within a year of their marriage or about 30 & the other couple long after at 60 years of age & that they were both married in one year, the Society must be a much greater gainer by the one than the other for they gain of the one 30 years payments more than the other. But to balance this its said that as they have the chance of gaining then they have the chance too of losing 30 years payments to the widow which is not in the others case and after all if you allow old people to enter within a year after their marriage its the same thing. So this is dubious or the question comes to this if you will allow men after a certain age 40 suppose to enter into the Society without a premium and what security the Society shall take to keep out old men that are dying.

9. The Society shall be constituted as soon as there are 20 adventurers.

10. Every adventurer shall have an equal vote.

11. The management of the Society shall be in this manner there shall be 30 Directors (7 to be a quorum) their office to go by rotation according to their standing in the Society the Directors to change every year except the one half who shall continue 2 years the Directors to keep books to ly open to all in the Society the old Directors to clear accounts with the new: all the Society to have a meeting once a year upon a fixed day & nothing to be determined at that meeting as a rule that shall not be carried by two thirds or three fourths of the whole. The Directors to serve gratis and the Clerks Cashiers etc. only to be payed.

12. The Society at first must be voluntary and therefore there must be no compulsitor on any to continue his payments, but in case any man do not pay his annual sum within 6 months after it is due he shall forfeit all preceding payments and his widow to have no jointure but the Society is to endeavour to obtain a charter from the Crown or act of Parliament as soon as possible.

13. No man nor his widow shall have it in his power to transfer his or her right to the jointure, to prevent stock jobbing.

14. If a man dy intestate and his widow marry her jointure shall be divided equally among his children, & she shall lose all title; but if he have no children the widow shall preserve a right to her jointure tho' she marry.

15.   A man shall have it in his power by testament to proportion the widows jointure betwixt her and his children as he pleases, or to give it to the children alone and his testament shall be a rule to the Society.

16.   When a mans wife dies he will doubtless discontinue his payments and if he marry again he must make a new bargain (if he would enter into the Society again) according to the above rules.

17.   The Society is not to have a great capital stock but to depend chiefly on their annual payments and not upon rents of land or interests of money but as they must have some capital especially at first, the securing & disposing of this capital to be left to the Court of Directors.

18.   The number of the Society not to be limited.

19.   If one has once entered into the Society & is to pay so much & afterwards thinks it fit to pay more that his widow may get a greater jointure he must not be allowed to do this without a great premium.

A p p e n d i x   I I

There is in the records of the Fund a sheet of calculations with the title "Tables for the Widows Scheme 1743." There is a note in Wallace's handwriting "I think they were made by Mr. Colin Maclaurin."

The headings of the Tables give an indication of the nature of the calculations:

Table 1. Showing the Progress of the Fund according to the Doctrine of Chance. On supposition that Ministers now marryed or haveing children and those hereafter marrying pay for once a Double Tax and also that the 18 Widows left annually be of 50 years of age but the other provisions to be the same as in the Scheme.

Table 2. Showing the progress of the fund on supposition that the Taxes on all Benefices are doubled the first year and on all those who marry for the first year of their marriage and that all children receive only half of the Provisions stated in the Scheme for the first 5 years and $\frac{3}{4}$ of the provisions for the next five years of the scheme and that the widows receive no annuity for the first year of their widowhood.

Note: The calculations showed that according to Table 1 the Fund might run into difficulty in the 21st. year but that under the arrangement of Table 2 the Fund should be sufficient at all times.

A p p e n d i x   I I I

Letter of Colin Maclaurin to the Reverend Mr. Robert Wallace, Moderator of the General Assembly of the Church of Scotland.

May 23, 1743

As you was pleased to mention my opinion concerning the scheme for providing an annuity to ministers widows and a stock for their children, in the committee of the general Assembly, I therefore thought it my duty to go over those computations again with care and lay the result fully before you to prevent mistakes of any kind. The design is so good that minute objections against the absolute perfection of the sheme or minute alterations seem to me to be improper, especially since it has been now so long under your consideration, and therefore I shall take notice only of what seems to me to be of importance and may easily be amended.

You was in the right, Sir, to represent me as a friend to the scheme in general. It must be advantageous to the body of ministers complexly taken because of the Tax on vacancies which I am confident on good grounds will amount to more than is supposed in the scheme. It must be advantageous on a second account to the widows and children of ministers because the annual tax is payable not only by those who shall leave a widow or children but likewise by those who shall leave neither. It must be advantageous because a greater improvement can be made of large sums and with less danger from the hazards to which all things are subjected by faithfull Trustees than of small annual sums by single ministers; as it is a certain rule that no single man unless he be extremely rich, ought to deal in Insurance but rich men or companies of men only; because loss to a poor man is more sensible than an equal gain. For these and other reasons too tedious to mention here I am of opinion that if this scheme take place and be faithfully executed as there is all the reason in the world to expect, it must be advantageous to the whole body of ministers and therefore if it be made equal it must be advantageous to every individual, those only expected who think they have no chance to leave a widow or child behind them. And as they must be few in number so they can only complain that they do for their brethren what they would have done for them if it had been their lot to have had their circumstances exchanged. The scheme is remarkably advantageous to the old and very few are so young as to have much reason to complain.

I was at a loss till Friday to know which scheme I was to compute, having already made several calculations that were rendered fruitless by subsequent alterations. But now I am obliged to acknowledge that I find great reason to conclude that the capital of 50000L.St. will not advance so fast as is supposed in the calculations of the scheme. I am obliged to justify the Accomptant who appears to have carried them out with skill and care upon the principles given to him. But the mistake lyes in the manner of bringing up the number of widows. It is said that one of the widows dyes out of 17 but for the greater certainty one of 18 only is supposed to dye. Now it is certain that one canot reasonably be expected to dye out of 18 till the age of 66 years, from registers that have been kept for a century of years of persons of 50 years of age one only dyes out of 31 yearly.

At first I did not imagine this would have so great an effect upon the progress of the Capital. I did observe to some Reverend ministers on Friday that it would retard its advancement considerably; but on going through the computations with care, I now find that supposing the Tax and provisions to stand as in the latter Table of the scheme (wherein the Tax on those now married and that have children and those that afterwards shall marry is supposed to be doubled) the stock will arise in the 21st. year to 33070:00:09 but in the 22nd. year will advance only to 33133:07:00 which increase for that year is of 63:06:03 only. Therefore in order to add 200L.St. to the Stock this year an abatement must be made from the provisions for this 22nd. year.

This conclusion is founded on the supposition that the 18 widows who are left yearly may be reckoned to be of 50 years of age at a medium. If we pitch upon 47 or 48 as a proper medium the Stock will be at a stand sooner or in a less number of years and the abatements from the provisions will be necessary sooner. But if we take a higher number than 50 for a medium of their ages the abatements will not come so soon. It is true that if their number when full was at a medium 306 we might suppose 51 to be the just medium of their ages when they are left widows but since it is advanced Principles and Data page 6 that the widows are left one with another between the age of 45 and 50 I could not venture to take a higher number than 50 and since the number of widows at present is no more than 304 I did not think it necessary to take a higher number than 50.

If the stock came to a stand in the 22nd. year when it is more than 33100L.St. it is evident that the abatements on the provisions must be continued for a great number of years to allow it to rise to 50,000L.St. by the addition of 200L per annum only.

To prevent this and its disagreeable consequences may I presume to propose 1. that the first year's tax be double not only on those ministers who are already married or have children but on all the benefices. 2. That the annuity be not payable to widows for the first year of their widowhood, because unless a minister at his death be in more debt to your fund than he can pay (which must be a rare case, and something surely must be left to your compassion and tenderness for one another) the ann may be supposed to afford as large a supply for the first year as the annuity for subsequent years. In like manner no annuity ought to be payed to the widows of such as bear offices in the Universities (tho' their successors may be taxed so as that there be no vacation of the tax) for the first year.

It is with reluctance that I propose this last but you will be pleased to observe that it is only one half year of annuity less than in the scheme and it is compensated by the benefit from the former article. I was the rather inclined to propose the first, because there is ground to suspect that 800 ministers which are supposed to be married or have children is too large a number: and if there be fewer in those circumstances the scheme will suffer by it. Besides to most of them it is only an anticipation of the time of payment that is proposed, I mean to such as are to marry.

I hope the liberty of proposing those things to you will be excused since it proceeds from a sincere concern for your success in so good a design and you can best judge whether these things are proper to be mentioned to the General Assembly.

I have begun the computation of the effect these articles would have on the scheme but have not had time to finish it. I have ground to think from what I have done that these (or any other equivalent to favour the rising of the capital) will in great measure answer the end.

What I have thought necessary to be represented to you on this occasion hinders not the scheme from being beneficial for the reasons above mentioned. It will be no difficult matter to satisfy any that are concerned that the computations are just and I shall readily wait on any you will be pleased to appoint for that purpose. It is only in the progress of the number of widows that I differ from the scheme; in everything else I retain the same numbers, I sincerely wish you success and am with the greatest regards

Your most obedient
Humble Servant
Colin Maclaurin

Coll. of Edinburgh
May 23, 1743.

P.S. The Table I have made of the number of widows and of the progress of the capital by which it appears to be stationary about the 22nd. year when no more than 31330L. is ready to be produced.

For the satisfaction of such as desyre it I have copied on

this leaf the number of widows in life entituled to the provisions according to the scheme and according to the Doctrine of chances (or Observations from Experience concerning the probabilities of Life) for some of the years.

Years of the Scheme	Widows in Life by the Scheme	Widows in life by the doctrine of chances, supposing them at a medium to be left at 50 years of age
12	152.27	179.64
17	193	231.85
20	212.17	257.12
25	238	288.33
30	257.11	306.60

A p p e n d i x   I V

Letter from Colin Maclaurin 24th May 1743 *to The Reverend Mr Robert Wallace Minister of the Gospell at Edinburgh*

I kept no copies of the letters I wrote to you yesterday having been wholly employed in pursuing the calculations and revising them but want to have copies for which purpose please either to return them or get them copied for me by one of your sons today. As you have increased your capital to 55,000L. (which by the by surprised me) and after all you have done it will hardly rise to 41,000 without making abatements necessary surely you ought to project some further remedy. The third article you and Mr. Webster would not allow me to mention was really more equitable than the first. You may think of it again in this shape, that for the first 4 years the children shall have only the half of the provisions stated in the scheme and for the next 4 years only three fourths of the same. If you think this a likely method I shall calculate its effect, I imagine you ought to have a probable scheme to show of the rising of the capital.

C. M. L.

May 24, 1743

I should be glad to have a copy today. I expect you will print nothing about my letters till I see it.

Appendix V

The following letter from Colin Maclaurin to Wallace is clearly a form of certificate intended for publication. From the wording of the letter it would appear that the Church had asked Maclaurin for his opinion:

Having considered the scheme for providing an annuity for minister's widows and a stock for their children laid before the late general Assembly the 12th. of May 1743 together with the alterations and amendments made upon the same by the genl. Assembly and my opinion being desired concerning the whole, I think myself obliged to say that the Design is so good that minute objections against the absolute perfection of the scheme seem to be improper after it has been so long under consideration and only observe that I have reason to be apprehensive that the capital will not rise so fast as is supposed in the scheme without deductions from the provisions proposed for the children. And as I am of the opinion that some deductions will be necessary in order that the proposed capital may be completed so it is most equitable that they should take place at the beginning of the scheme when they will have the greatest effect to promote the advancement of the capital and will require to be continued for a smaller number of years. The provisions however supposing these deductions to be allowed will be still abundantly advantageous. It is evident that this scheme must be advantageous to the Body of ministers taken complexely because of the tax on vacancies which I have reason to think will amount to more than is supposed in the scheme. It must be advantageous to the widows & children of ministers on a second account because the taxes are supposed to be payable not only by those who shall leave widows or children but likewise by such as shall leave neither. It must also be advantageous because a greater improvement may be made of large sums by faithfull Trustees and with less danger from the Hazards to which all things of this nature are subjected than of small annual sums by single ministers. For these and other reasons which it would be tedious to describe here at length I sincerely wish well to this design and cannot but be of opinion that if the scheme take place and be faithfully executed (as there is all the reason in the world to expect) it will prevent the unhappy circumstances to which ministers' widows and children are too often reduced. It is remarkably advantageous to those ministers who are advanced in years and they only seem to have any ground to complain of it who think they have no chance to leave a widow or child behind them. But as these are few in number so it can only be said that they shall do for their Brethren what their Brethren must have done for them if it had been their lot to have had their circumstances exchanged.

Colin Maclaurin

College of Edinburgh
   June 3, 1743

CHAPTER 3

The Scottish Ministers' Widows'
Fund of 1744

The Earliest Actuarially-based Fund in the World

David J P Hare BSc PhD FFA
and *William F Scott* MA PhD FFA

The previous contributions by Mr Dunlop[1] and Mr Dow[2] have already clearly described the chain of events which resulted in the setting up of this Widows' Fund, as well as its early history. It is the purpose of this chapter to discuss the various calculations upon which the Scheme was based, and to show that it may rightly be said to be the first actuarially-based fund in the world.

Much of the early work of investigating human mortality (i.e. the likelihood, or probability, of dying at any given age last birthday), and how these statistics could be used in the pricing of annuities, was carried out in Holland in the second half of the 17th century.[3] (An annuity is a series of level payments continuing so long as a specified person—the annuitant—survives.) These early calculations (by Christiaan and Lodewiik Huygens, de Witt and others) employed correct principles of probability to suggest suitable prices for the annuities sold by states and towns, usually to help to pay the costs of wars.

In 1693 the famous astronomer Edmund Halley constructed the first comprehensive published life table, based on the experience of the city of Breslau (see References [4, 5, 6] and Illustration 4). We shall later show that this life table played a very significant role in the foundation and early development of the Scottish Ministers' Widows' Fund. (By a life table we mean a set of figures, denoted by 1_x, one for each age, x, which represent the number of lives who are expected to live to age x out of an initial group at some starting age. These figures may then be used to calculate the probability of death and survival at each age covered by the table, as well as expectations of life and how the cost of a life annuity or life assurance policy should vary with the age of the would-be annuitant or assured life.)

Halley was secretary of the Royal Society and editor of its journal, the *Philosophical Transactions*. The Society had received data consisting of the numbers of births and deaths at the city of Breslau for each month in the five year period 1687 to 1691, classified according to sex and for the deaths also by age, from the Lutheran pastor Caspar Neumann. Halley was asked to analyse this data in an attempt to use it in the pricing of life annuities, and in 1693 presented a paper summarising his results. From our point of view, the most important feature of this research was the appearance of the first comprehensive published life table—earlier tables, such as that of Graunt, were very brief or were unpublished. Halley also calculated annuity values, using his own life table, on correct principles. (The English government, however, continued to sell annuities at arbitrary and unsound prices.)

In order that a fund (that is, an institution, such as a pension scheme or life assurance society, which accumulates money from contributions and investments to pay for benefits and expenses depending on the death or survival of specified lives) may be described as "actuarially-based", it must give due regard to the following factors:

1. the mortality rates of the lives involved;
2. the rate of interest likely to be earned on the fund's investments; and
3. the expenses of management.

In addition, the fund may have to pay attention to other factors such as marriage rates (if the benefits depend on marital status), and to be aware of the possibility of options against the fund. For example, if members (or prospective members) are given a choice of a large or a small death benefit, with a corresponding premium, the healthier lives may tend to choose the small benefit, may while unhealthy lives tend to choose the large benefit.

It is our contention that the Ministers' Widows' Scheme is an actuarially-based fund, and that no others predate it. In order to support these statements, we shall describe the principles and calculations upon which the Scheme was based.

The main proponents of the plan, the Edinburgh ministers Robert Wallace and Alexander Webster, based most of their calculations on statistics concerning the average annual numbers of ministers, ministers' widows, deaths of ministers leaving widows, ministers leaving children but no widow, and so on. As the annual contribution income from the ministers would at first exceed the benefit and expense payments, a fund would be built up; when the number of widows reached its maximum (or stationary) level, the interest on the fund would pay the difference between the benefit and expense outgo and the contribution income. This type of scheme is referred to as a "maximum" plan, and is perfectly sound in the circumstances for which it was designed: that is, when there is a guaranteed annual income from contributors, benefits gradually increase to a stationary level, and funds can be securely invested at a known rate of interest. The rate of contribution, such details of the scheme as marriage-taxes, and the provision for children, must be correctly calculated, using compound interest and appropriate mortality tables: if not, the fund will continue to grow after the benefits have reached their maximum level, or it will grow for a few years and then decline rapidly.

The plan devised by Wallace and Webster was put to the General Assembly on 14th May 1742 in an amended form, and the General Assembly sent it for consideration by Presbyteries, who had to report to the Commission in November. The Commission modified the scheme again, and by May 1743 a "Rectified Scheme"[7] was ready to be put forward to the General Assembly (see Illustration 1). The calculations are to be found in a paper printed on 4th May 1743[8] and were probably the work of Wallace (but perhaps Wallace and Webster).

The calculations fall into two parts, the first stage being directed towards estimating the size of fund which would ultimately be required if the contribution and benefit rates were as follows:

Class	Annual Contribution	Widow's Annual Annuity
1	£2.12.06	£10
2	£3.18.09	£15
3	£5.05.00	£20
4	£6.11.03	£25

The originators of the Fund would appear to have been aware that the subscription rates should have increased with age at entry, as there was some later criticism of those older ministers who chose the highest rates of benefit, but uniform premium rates were preferred, probably for reasons of administrative simplicity and because, in future, nearly all the entrants would be young. A key feature of the Scheme was that membership was voluntary for existing ministers but compulsory for all later entrants.

It was assumed that all 930 ministers would join the Scheme and that the numbers choosing classes 1 to 4 would be 200, 500, 200 and 30 respectively. It was further assumed that the number of contributors, and the distribution across the different classes, would remain constant and so apply in the stationary population which would eventually be reached. The eventual annual number of widows' annuities was taken to be 300, this being divided among the four classes in the same proportions as the contributors.

Thus the average contribution per minister was taken to be £4.00.05, with an average widow's annuity of £15.06.06 per annum. The forty vacancies (and this number was also assumed to remain constant) were each assumed to contribute £5 per annum, so the eventual contribution income, ignoring marriage-taxes, was taken to be £3,940.12.06.

The eventual annual outgo was estimated to be as follows:

	£
Payments to 300 widows	4,596.13.04
Payments to 5 families whose fathers die without a widow, each family receiving 10 years' annuity	766.06.00

Payments to 2 families left with a stepmother, each family receiving 5 years' annuity	153.05.00
Payments to 3 families whose mothers (being annuitants) die or remarry, each family being taken to receive 5 years' annuity	229.17.06
Expenses (collector's salary, etc.)	200.00.00
	£5,946.00.00 approx.

Thus the eventual annual expenditure was expected to exceed the annual contribution income by £2,000; so, on the basis of interest at a rate of 4% per annum, a fund of £50,000 would be required to meet the eventual shortfall.

The next stage of the calculations involved the estimation of the cash flows in the early years of the Scheme in order to determine whether the fund would increase to this desired level. Before going on to consider this, it is worth investigating further the reasoning which lay behind some of the assumptions mentioned above.

Dow has already described how Wallace had received statistics from Presbyteries regarding the numbers of ministers' deaths, widows, children, etc. in the period from March 1722 to March 1742. It comes as no surprise, therefore, to read that:

"The foregoing Provisions are proposed; because 'tis found by a Medium of 20 years back, that 27 Ministers die yearly, 18 of them leave Widows, 5 of them Children without a Widow, 2 of them who leave Widows, leave also Children of a former Marriage, under the Age of 16; and when the whole Number of Widows shall be complete, 3 Annuitants will die, or marry, leaving Children under 16."

It was also noted that:

"The Medium, taken from the 20 years last past, cannot be reckoned too favourable for the Scheme; in Regard, that the greater Part of Ministers settled at, or a little after the Revolution, were then become old, and have died in this Period; Besides, we are informed that some who have made accurate observations, as to the Death of Ministers in different Periods, find the above Medium just."

In other words, it was considered that, on account of the special nature of the population of ministers at that time, basing future mortality rates on the experience of the previous twenty years should result in overstating the numbers of deaths (and hence the numbers of new widows and amounts of annuity benefit to be paid).

It is also interesting to see how the number of 300 widows was arrived at:

"With respect to the number (of widows) provided for at length, it may be observed, that it being about 55 years since the Revolution, and that the whole Ministers, once in the Church, have died out since that time, one or two excepted, the highest number of widows must be supposed now on life; and as therefore at present 304, 'tis from thence reasonably concluded, that if present incumbents, or those hereafter to be ordained, marry, in the same proportion, there will at length be the same number of their widows on life at one time."

In other words, sufficient time has elapsed since the Revolution of 1688 for the number of ministers' widows to have reached its stationary level; the maximum number of widows to be supported is therefore equal to the current number of ministers' widows.

The figure of 300 was justified further by means of rough calculations on the basis of expected lifetimes. It was noted that, on average, ministers died leaving widows aged between 45 and 50 and that, "according to the exactist computations", such widows could be expected to live for another 17 years. (This was confirmed by the fact that there were very few widows then alive whose husbands had died more than twenty years before.) It therefore followed that if all the eighteen new widows each year were to live a further 17 years, then, when the stationary population was reached, it could be expected that 306 (i.e. 18×17) widows would be alive at any one time.

Various other comments were made concerning the experience which might be expected regarding the numbers of widows and other dependants, and the associated benefit outflow, especially where it was thought that the assumptions underlying the calculations erred on the side of caution. But the above extracts are sufficient to demonstrate that "primitive" actuarial principles were indeed being put into practice in the development of the Scheme; on the other hand, the degree of refinement shown in Maclaurin's calculations, which we shall discuss later, is not present.

Calculations were carried out for two variations of the Rectified Scheme. In the first variation there was no marriage tax, but widows' benefits were reduced in the early years of membership. In the second variation, however, there was a marriage-tax equal to one year's contributions (not widow's annuity), payable by those who were married or had children when they joined the Scheme and on future marriages of members. On the other hand, no deductions were to be made from the benefits if the contributions paid prior to death amounted to less than three years' widow's annuity. Let us study this second variation of the Scheme, upon which Maclaurin based his remarks and calculations of 23rd May 1743.

As noted above, the purpose of this second stage of the calculations was to estimate the expected cash flows in the early years of the Scheme and so demonstrate that the fund would, indeed, increase to the desired level of £50,000. These calculation were based upon the following formula:

Fund at end of year = Fund at start of year
+ contribution income
+ investment income
− benefit outgo − expenses

The contribution income came from two sources: "normal" contributions and marriage-taxes. We have already dealt with the calculation of the former: it was assumed that the level of contribution income would remain constant from year to year. As regards the expected income from marriage-taxes, it may be deduced from Wallace's cash flow projections and a letter from Maclaurin to Wallace[9] that it was expected that in the first year, 800 ministers would pay the marriage-tax, and in each subsequent year it would be paid by 25 ministers.

The benefit outgo is made up of widows' annuities and children's benefits. The first item clearly depends upon the number of widows alive in any given year. We have already seen that it was assumed that 18 ministers would die each year leaving a widow, but, after 5 years (say) there would be no guarantee that all 90 widows would still be receiving benefit; some might have died and others might have remarried: these possibilities must be allowed for in the cash flow calculations. Wallace chose to assume a constant annual combined rate of mortality and remarriage for widows of 1/18. Thus, of the 18 widows present at the end of the first year, 17 were expected to be alive and receiving benefit at the end of the second year; these would be joined by 18 new widows, thereby making a total of 35. The survivors of these at the end of the third year were expected to number 33.06 (= 35 × (17/18)); another 18 join them, making a total of 51.06, and so on. Since a new widow was expected to receive on average half a year's benefits in the year in which her husband died, the cost of widow's benefits in the first year was reduced by half. The projected numbers and benefits in the first three years were thus taken to be as follows:

Year	Number of Widows	Annuity Outgo
1	18	£137.925
2	35	£398.450
3	51.06	£644.500

(The average widow's annuity was assumed to be £15.6.6, which is equivalent to £15.325 in decimal notation.)

The annual costs of children's benefits were then estimated. There was a constant total annual cost of 60 times the
average widow's annuity for children whose father died
leaving them no mother, or a stepmother. The calculation of
the total benefits to families of deceased annuitants allowed
for the number of widows dying each year and the average
number of annuity payments received by them. (The Scheme
included the provision that each family of children whose
mother died while an annuitant was to receive a lump sum
equal to the difference, if any, between 10 years' annuities
and the payments received by their mother.)

Wallace assumed that three families would be left each
year when 18 widows died annually, so 3/18 of widows would
die leaving a young family. Thus, the number of families left
in the second year was expected to be 3/18, while the
average number of annuity payments received by the widow
was taken as 1. (A widow who died in year 2 would have
received half a year's annuity in the year of her husband's
death, and half a year's annuity in the year of her own
death.) This would leave nine years' annuity as the average
benefit to the family, making a pay-out for this benefit in the
second year of one and a half times the average widow's
annuity (since $1.5 = 9 \times (3/18)$). This corresponds exactly
with the payment for year 2 in the published calculations
reproduced below. The average number of annuity payments to be received by each family was taken to be five
eventually.

The projected accounts for the first few years of the
Scheme were thus as follows:

						Fund at end of previous year, plus	
	Contribution income from:			*Outgo for:*			
Year	Normal Contributions	Marriage-Taxes	Widows' Annuities	Children's Benefits	Expenses	Interest at 4%	Fund at end of year
1	3940.63	3216.662	137.925	919.500	200	0	5899.867
2	3940.63	104.507	398.450	942.495	200	6135.862	8640.062
3	3940.63	100.518	644.500	961.750	200	8985.664	11220.562
4	3940.63	100.519	876.925	977.650	200	11669.384	13655.958

(The figure of £104.507 from marriage-taxes in the second year appears to be too high by £3.989. In Maclaurin's calculations of 23rd May 1743 this value is replaced by £101.518, so it may have been a mistake.)

Two aspects of the scheme are worthy of note here. The projected expenses of £200 per annum were relatively modest, and the first £30,000 of capital investment of the Scheme was to consist of *compulsory* loans to the ministers, in a prescribed order. Interest was to be paid at 4% per annum (the rate assumed in the calculations for the Scheme), with the capital repayable on death. In this respect the Scheme bears some resemblance to a modern credit union.

An important assumption was that regarding the mortality of the main beneficiaries, the widows. It was important not to overstate their death rates, otherwise future benefit outflow would be underestimated. Ignoring remarriages, Wallace assumed that, on average, one widow in eighteen would die each year, and it was to this estimate that Colin Maclaurin, Professor of Mathematics at Edinburgh University, took exception.

In early May 1743, Maclaurin wrote that "Mr Wallace desires me to go over the computations for the Scheme", because "there are some wrong-headed people talk absurdly on the subject, which he imagines a paper from me would silence." Maclaurin's opinion may also have been sought by his colleagues at the University of Edinburgh, since the professors asked, on Thursday 19th May 1743, to be allowed to join the Scheme.

The course of events until Tuesday 24th May, is related by Maclaurin in a letter[10] to the Under-Secretary of State for Scotland, Sir Andrew Mitchell, which we reproduce here in full.

Dear Sir,

The week before the last my eldest boy fell ill of the small pox, and is now in a fair way of recovery. Having discovered a very material error by which it appeared that the Capital of 5000 L.St. proposed in the Scheme for providing Ministers' Widows and a stock to their Children would in 22 years come to a stand and not rise above

31000 L.St. without abating from the Provisions, I was obliged to represent this to the General Assembly, and having proposed three Articles to favour the rising of the Capital to Mess Wallace & Webster they would not permit me to propose the third to the Assembly tho' the most considerable and equitable lest it should give a handle to those who were against the Scheme. The two I proposed were agreed to, but these will only raise the Capital to about 41000 L.St. The third was, that for the first 3 or 4 years of the Scheme Ministers' children should receive only a part of the provision stated there. Nor could they complain that by paying 5 guineas for one year or two only their children should receive only 100 L.St. (instead of 200) at the beginning of the Scheme. But tho' I dealt with Mess W W not to mince the Matter but set it fairly before the Assembly, they from reasons of Management would not, and all they would suffer me to put into my letter was that something still would be requisite to raise the Capital. How without providing for this they raised their Capital yesterday to 55000 is to me strange, nor have I had an Opportunity to expostulate with them.

Till Friday I kneu not what I was to compute because of their perpetual alterations. After Friday I laboured day and night till I have put myself so much out of order that I was obliged this day to lye down to sleep. I have got their Capital better'd by 8000L and 'tis not my fault that they have not put it into such a shape as to anseur. I shall send you a copy of my letter when I get it from Mr Wallace, for I had so litle time to spare from the computations that I could not take a copy. I imagined that the pains I took in this affair would not be acceptable to you, as I am now in a condition to make you able to judge of it easily, and it may be one of the most important affairs may come before you from this Country. My son's illness made it impossible for me to go hitherto, and I could not have left this affair easily after so many had called upon me to give my opinion, and my opinion was even mentioned in the Assembly without my leave.

Unluckily my farm is not set but waste. If this misfortune can be remedied I am to set out in a few days. The delay is not from choice but unavoidable and unforeseen accidents. Meantime, Dear Sir, excuse this Scrawl writ in the utmost hurry by Your Aff frd.

Edr. May 24   *C.M.L.*
    1743   next post expect to hear more fully.

We shall discuss Maclaurin's calculations more fully below, but let us first summarise the progress of the Scheme from May 1743 until it became law the following year.

The General Assembly began to meet on Thursday, 12th May 1743, and Wallace was elected Moderator. Following a debate on 19th May the Assembly approved the Scheme and decided that the professors of the Scottish Universities should be allowed to join. (When the Scheme became law in 1744, the professors at Edinburgh, Glasgow and St Andrews were included. Those at Aberdeen were included in the Scheme a little later.)

The Scheme was remitted to the Commission with an instruction to apply for an Act of Parliament, but at this stage some of its provisions were subject to variation, as the Scheme put into effect by the 1744 Act differs slightly from the version given in a pamphlet describing the Scheme as "past and resolved" by the General Assembly.[12]

Wallace and Maclaurin continued to correspond about the Scheme's finances, and a letter from Maclaurin to Wallace, dated 3rd June, appears on the final page of the pamphlet mentioned above. In this letter, reproduced by Dow (see Reference 2, Appendix I), Maclaurin expressed his general support for the Scheme, but suggested that some action, such as reducing the children's benefits in the early years of the Scheme, would be necessary to stabilise its finances. (It seems likely that Wallace and Webster no longer objected to publishing a letter by Maclaurin making the suggestion that children's benefits should be reduced, as the Scheme had gone through the General Assembly.) There was perhaps a tacit understanding by the Commission that something would be done to improve the Scheme's finances before it passed into law.

The rapid progress of the Scheme from May 1743 until

2nd March 1744, when it became law, is described by Dunlop and Dow. Maclaurin's support for the Scheme was one of the factors which helped to smooth the path. Of course, political factors played a considerable part—Wallace was in favour with the government of the time—but it seems that the financial soundness of the Scheme did help. The Act of 1744 (17 Geo II cap. 11) received the royal assent on 2nd March 1744 and came into effect on 25th March 1744.

The version of the Scheme enacted in 1744 differed from the second variation of the Rectified Scheme of 1743 in that there were no payments to children left with a stepmother, and all those present at the start of the Scheme had to pay the marriage-tax. Expenses were not to exceed £210 per annum (this was, of course, a very modest proportion of the annual contribution income of the Scheme) and, largely in view of the fact that professors were now eligible to join, the maximum capital was increased to about £65,000.

But let us now return to the calculations which Maclaurin sent to Robert Wallace on 23rd May 1743.[13] These are almost certainly the earliest actuarially-correct fund calculations ever carried out, if to be "actuarially-correct" requires (inter alia) the use of a realistic and accurate life table. (We exclude annuity calculations as not relating to a continuing fund.)

The "very material error" noticed by Maclaurin in Wallace's work was, as we have noted, the incorrect estimation of the numbers of widows. Wallace had based his projection of the number of beneficiaries on a constant mortality rate for widows of 1/18 per annum, thereby ignoring the varying age-distribution of the annuitants. Maclaurin pointed out that, according to Halley's life table for the city of Breslau, the average annual mortality rate of widows, at least in the early years of the Scheme, would not be as high as this. Maclaurin calculated the numbers of widows at the end of each year and on the assumption that the average age of the eighteen new widows each year was 50 and that their mortality followed Halley's table. The estimates of Maclaurin and Wallace for the first three years are shown below:

Number of widows receiving annuities:

Year	Maclaurin's estimate	Wallace's estimate
1	18	18
2	$18 + 17.42 = 35.42$	35
3	$18 + 17.42 + 16.85 = 52.27$	51.06

As this table shows, Maclaurin's estimates are rather higher than those of Wallace.

Maclaurin seems not to have adjusted the projected children's benefits (the financial effects being relatively small), nor any other item of the cash flow except the sum paid in marriage-taxes in year 2. He then carried out his own estimates of the future size of the Fund, using his own estimates of the numbers of widows in a table, which is reproduced in Illustration 2.

The implication of this adjustment was that instead of rising to £50,000, the capital would increase to only £33,133 (at time 22 years) and then decline. In order to protect the Scheme from the "disagreeable consequences", Maclaurin put forward the three suggestions mentioned in this letter to Sir Andrew Mitchell, and carried through calculations to show that if this or some equivalent action was taken the capital would rise to the desired level. (Incidentally, Maclaurin's projections show the number of widows rising to 313.62 by the end of the 35th year, which exceeds the maximum value of 300 assumed by Wallace.)

At this point we raise a possible criticism of the Scheme's financial basis: that it did not allow for its optional character, especially in respect of those present at inception were concerned. It may be that the originators (and Maclaurin) expected all the ministers to join, or not to act out of self-interest by (for example) selecting the largest annuity rate if they were old and likely to leave a young widow. In this the Scheme's originators were to be disappointed, but it appears that, given the uncertainties surrounding the numbers and ages of ministers who would join the various classes, the number who would decline to join, and the imperfections of the statistics from which the ultimate numbers of widows and children were estimated, it was thought best to get the Scheme enacted and to adjust its terms later, if necesary, by Act of Parliament.

Three years after its foundation (during which time the Scheme had successfully weathered the 1745 Rebellion), the Trustees decided to examine the Scheme's finances in detail. It was found—not surprisingly—that not all those eligible to join had done so, and that many of the older ministers had chosen the larger annuities. Detailed calculations were carried out by Webster, Lord Provost George Drummond, Maclaurin's successor Matthew Stewart, accountant Alexander Chalmers and possibly the Rev Alexander Bryce of Kirknewton, using Halley's life table for both the contributors and their widows. These calculations[14] (see Illustration 3) are the first actuarial valuation of a continuing fund ever published. (Maclaurin's calculations of 23rd May 1743 were not published.) It was found that the annual numbers of new widows and families left each year had been underestimated in the 1743 calculations, due to imperfect data having been received by Wallace and Webster. Cash flow projections were conducted using correct principles, making an allowance for the fact that 135 ministers had declined to join the Scheme at the outset. (No specific allowance was made for the facts that those who had joined might be more likely to be married than those who had declined, and that many elderly ministers had chosen the larger annuity rates, but these are perhaps rather refined points.)

As a consequence of this report, the Trustees asked and obtained permission from the General Assembly of 1748 to seek a new Act to amend the Scheme. The principal change was the introduction of the rule that widow's and children's benefits should be reduced if the contributions paid were less than three years' widow's annuity. The maximum permissible capital was raised to about £80,000 and there were other alterations.

These amendments were enacted in 1749 (22 Geo II cap. 21). The projections of the size of the Fund published in 1748 agreed very well with the actual values, at least for the next thirty years. After that time the actual Fund exceeded the projected, partly because of the effects of another

Act in 1778 and because of interest surpluses on some of its investments, but few modern financial institutions could claim such accuracy as was achieved in the world's first published actuarial valuation.

At this point let us pause to consider the appropriateness of Halley's Breslau table for eighteenth-century Scottish ministers and their widows. Since the Breslau table applied to the entire Lutheran population of that city towards the end of the 17th century, it might be expected that its mortality rates would be rather higher than those of Scottish ministers and their widows (who were, of course, a select group) some 50 years later. The records of the Scheme in the 18th century do not give the ages of the ministers or their widows, so no direct mortality study may be made, but there is some indirect evidence that they lived rather longer than Halley's table indicates.

In Wallace's calculations of 4th May 1743, it was assumed that 27 ministers would die each year and that the ministers formed a stationary population of size 930. If we suppose that 27 ministers joined at exact age 26 at the beginning of each year, and ignore resignations and deprivations, then according to Halley's table the ministers would form a stationary population numbering (at the beginning of each year):

$$\frac{27}{l_{26}} (l_{26} + l_{27} + \ldots) = 833.81$$

(We have continued Halley's table to age 99, using a suggested continuation[15].) This suggests that the mortality of Halley's table was too heavy for the ministers, and hence probably for their widows also.

Another piece of indirect evidence is provided by a study of French monks and nuns published by Deparcieux in 1747 (see Reference 6 – page 60). Their mortality was considerably lighter than that of Halley's life table.

Maclaurin's calculations of 23rd May 1743 made no assumptions about the mortality of the contributors, merely of their widows, and the fact that he ignored the possibility of remarriage of the widows made up, at least to some extent, for the use of the mortality table which was probably too heavy for the group under consideration. In the calculations for the Scheme in 1748, Halley's table was taken to apply to both contributors and widows: the net effect was probably to err on the side of caution in the Fund projections. One must, of course, remember that few other mortality tables existed at that time.

In his Report of 1862[16] Thomson investigated the mortality of the contributors and annuitants from 1843 to 1861, and found that the mortality of the contributors followed the Carlisle table (published in 1815 by Joshua Milne), while that of the annuitants was rather lower.

The investment policy for the Fund is also worthy of further comment. As mentioned above, the orginators of the Scheme planned to invest the first £30,000 or so of the capital in compulsory £30 loans to the contributors, in a set order. This method of investment did not, however, turn out to be as successful as had been hoped, although there may well have been many young ministers who were quite glad of their loans. Of the money lent to ministers between 1744 and 1779, when such loans were discontinued, a certain amount had to be written off. In the report of the Trustees for 1769,[17] for example, the Collector stated that the deposed minister of Durisdeer "went abroad to some of his Majesty's plantations, and has not since been heard of", and that there was no prospect of recovering the contributions lent by the Fund to this ex-minister. The Collector also quoted the case of another deposed minister, gone abroad, from whom the Fund was trying to recover its £30 loan and unpaid contributions by securing household effects.

Apart from these losses, it may also have been administratively complicated to have so many small loans, and from 1752 onwards the Scheme invested in landed property, obtaining a rate of interest of $4\frac{1}{2}\%$ per annum until 1816. During the next 78 years, the rate of interest on these loans varied between $3\frac{1}{2}\%$ and 5%.[18]

Webster continued to take a close interest in the affairs of the Fund, and in 1773 he made some suggestions which led to a new act in 1779 (19 Geo. III cap. 20). The main changes were that the £30 loans to contributors were discontinued, new entrants aged over 40 had to pay a marriage-tax of two and a half times the annual contribution if they were married or had children, and the maximum capital was raised to £100,000.

The fact that the rate of interest on landed property was above 4% per annum helped the capital to grow, and towards the end of the 18th century the capital exceeded £100,000. In 1801 it was decided to keep the capital of the main Scheme fixed at £100,000, to place £2,814 in a Reserve Fund and to distribute surplus by increasing the benefits. There followed a period of inflation during the Napoleonic wars, and in 1814 the contributions were increased by 20% (this being optional for existing members but compulsory for future entrants) and two New Funds were created. Annuity payments were increased in stages, and from 1826 to 1843 the Fund remained in a fairly stable position, with a total capital of about £167,000.

It is hoped that we have clearly demonstrated that the Scottish Ministers' Widows' Fund has been actuarially-based since its inception. In order to show that it is the oldest such fund in the world it is necessary to demonstrate that no others predate it.

Inquiries to Germany, Denmark, Sweden, Holland and elsewhere have failed to find any actuarially-based financial institution established before 1744. As for Britain, one possible contender is the Widows' Scheme, aimed primarily at Church of England clergy, set up by the Mercers' Company in 1699. This scheme had the same single premium, or annual premium ceasing at age 60, for all entrants (the maximum entry age being reduced to 50 in 1717). Since entry to the Scheme was optional, there were many old entrants with much younger wives, and problems were compounded by falls in the rate of interest. Annuity payments were reduced, and eventually the scheme had to be bailed out by a government subsidy. In view of these failings— particularly the failure to allow for the optional nature of membership—this scheme cannot be considered to be actuarially sound. The Scottish Ministers' Widows' Scheme predates the world's first indisputably actuarially-based life office, the Equitable, which was founded in 1762. We also remark that the Scheme is mentioned by Hald (see Reference 3) in his history of life insurance mathematics.

Finally, we refer the reader to previous studies of the origins of the Scheme by Deuchar,[19] who carried out calculations along the lines he supposed were followed by Webster, and Winsor,[20] who also considered the contributions of Wallace to demography. An earlier study of the Scheme is that by Wilkie,[21] a minister of the parish of Cults, who included a Dissertation addressed to the Trustees suggesting ways to distribute the capital when it exceeded £100,000. The Scheme is also mentioned by other writers on Widows' Funds, including Hine.[22]

We should like to thank Professor A Hald, Mr Christopher Lewin and Mr Trevor Sibbett for careful comments on aspects of this study.

References

1   A I Dunlop: *Provision for Ministers' Widows in Scotland—Eighteenth Century*. Records of the Church History Society XVII, pp 233–248, 1971. (Reproduced as Chapter 1 of this book.)

2   J B Dow: *Early Actuarial Work in Eighteenth Century Scotland.* TFA 33, pp 193–299, with discussion, 1975. (Reproduced as Chapter 2 of this book.)

3   A Hald: *A History of Probability and Statistics and their applications before 1750*, John Wiley & Sons, New York.

4   E Halley: "An Estimate of the Degrees of Mortality", *Philosophical Transactions* 17, pp 596, 654, 1693.

5   G Heywood, *Edmund Halley: Astronomer and Actuary,* JIA 112, 279, 1985.

6   Major Greenwood: *Medical Statistics from Graunt to Farr*, Cambridge University Press, 1948.

7   *Representation and Scheme for providing an annuity*: R Fleming and Co, Edinburgh, 12th May 1743: CH9/17/1.

8   "Principles and Data. On which the Calculation is instituted, relating to the Rectified Scheme, etc as varied by the Commission in March last. At Edinburgh, 4th May 1743." Institute of Actuaries' Library D658. This paper, with the final two pages omitted, is also in CH9/17/1.

9   Letter from Colin Maclaurin to Revd Robert Wallace, 23rd May 1743. CH9/17/16. Reproduced by Dow (1: Appendix III) and

Mills (11: letter 76). Mills incorrectly states that the original manuscript is lost.

10 S Mills: ibid. Letter from Colin Maclaurin to Sir Andrew Mitchell, 24th May 1743. D M Add. Ms 6861 f 54. Reproduced by Mills (11: letter 78).

11 S Mills: *The collected letters of Colin Maclaurin*, Shiva Publishing, Cheshire, 1982.

12 "Scheme for providing an annuity ... past and resolved by the General Assembly of the Church of Scotland, met at Edinburgh on the 12th May 1743": R Fleming & Co, Edinburgh: CH9/7/2.

13 CH9/17/16.

14 "Calculations with the principles and data on which they were instituted ... showing the rise and progress of the fund": T Lumsden, Edinburgh, 1748: CH9/17/34.

15 H Braun: *Urkunden und Materialien zur Geschichte der Lebensversicherung und der Lebensversicherungstechnik*, E S Mittler and Sohn, Berlin, 1937.

16 W T Thomson: *Report upon the Fund*, R and R Clark, Edinburgh, 1862.

17 *Reports on the Ministers' Widows' Fund, 1749-1821*, New College Library, University of Edinburgh.

18 D P Paulin: "Life Office Investments, Retrospect and Outlook", in Transactions of the Actuarial Society of Edinburgh III, pp 229-259, 1896 (Graph).

19 D Deuchar: "Notes on Widows' Fund" in Transactions of the Actuarial Society of Edinburgh III, pp 197-227, 1896.

20 M P Winsor: *Robert Wallace, Demographer*, A B Thesis, Harvard University, 1965.

21 D Wilkie: *Theory of Interest, Simple and Compound, Derived from First Principles and applied to Annuities*, Peter Hill, Edinburgh, 1794, chap IX.

22 D R W Hine: *Valuation of Widows' Funds*, R Grant & Sons, London, 1868.

I l l u s t r a t i o n s

[*These illustrations appear with other examples in the mid-section of the book.*]

1 *Representation and Scheme for providing an Annuity:* This is the title page of a pamphlet describing the Scheme and offering it for consideration by the General Assembly in May 1743.

2 *The Widows' Scheme:* Colin Maclaurin's calculations of 23rd May 1743. These are the first actuarially-correct continuing fund calculations in the world.

3 *Calculations with Principles and Data* .... The title page of the first "actuarial report" ever published, 1748.

4 *Mr Halley's Table:* Edmund Halley's famous life table, 1693, as it appears in *Calculations with Principles and Data* .... (see Illustration 3).

CHAPTER 4

Notes on the Fund
in the First Hundred Years

A Ian Dunlop TD MA BD
and *George C Philip* FFA

[For Acts of Parliament, see Appendix 1, pp 135-146. The date is the Year of the Act's receiving the Royal Assent.]

In 1779 the trustees published *An Account of the Rise and Nature of the Fund Established by Act of Parliament*, an abridgement of the first two statutes and copies of papers relative to the Fund.

In the first Act (1744) the first trustees are named; beginning with Mr Neil McVicar of the West Kirk of Edinburgh (St Cuthbert's) and the other Edinburgh ministers. The Edinburgh ministers continued to play an important part in the work of the Fund. The first meetings were in the aisle of the Old Kirk in St Giles' and then in new offices in Scot's Close. By the time of the Disruption in 1843 the meetings were at 6 North St David Street. Stated meetings took place on the second Tuesday of February, March, May and November. The trustees chose their own preses, one of the first of whom was George Wishart of Edinburgh Tron, who went with Wallace to London to ask for the Act of Parliament in 1743. He was Clerk of the General Assembly and died in 1785. Nine trustees constituted a quorum.

The trustees were to appoint a *Clerk* at not more than £50 p/a and an officer at not more than £5 p/a. The principal appointment, however, was that of *Collector* with a salary of £155 p/a. He would keep all accounts, ensure all contributions, which were prior debts, and he was given power to apply for letters of horning. He was responsible for making

77

all payments and had to take a personal bond for £7000. Payments were to be made in May and accounts prepared yearly. The Collector's appointment had to be approved by the General Assembly. Each year the trustees had to report to the Assembly.

We learn from "Jupiter" Carlyle's *Autobiography* that the first Collector was Mr James Stewart, Attorney in Exchequer (p. 241). He also tells us that Stewart's successor, in 1771, was Alexander Webster of the Tolbooth, one of the founders of the Scheme. Carlyle makes it clear that he did not like Webster, who, he wrote, was very short of money and sought the salary of Collector. When Webster died in 1784 joint collectors were appointed; James MacKnight of Edinburgh Old Kirk and the very distinguished Sir Henry Moncreiff Wellwood, Bart, of St Cuthbert's. From then on for some time, the office of Collector seems to have been a kind of "plum" ministerial appointment. MacKnight died in 1800, but Moncreiff continued until he died in 1827, when the General Assembly recorded four pages of appreciation of his services. His successor was Andrew Grant of Edinburgh St Andrew's. He held joint appointment with Principal Nicoll of United College, St Andrews, until Nicoll died in 1835. Nicoll had been responsible for considerable improvement of the Scheme in 1814. When Grant died in 1836 he was succeeded by Robert Gordon of the High Kirk of Edinburgh. Gordon joined the Free Church at the Disruption in 1843, but carried on as Collector until he reported to the General Assembly of 1844. James Grant of St Mary's Edinburgh was then appointed.

A completely new Act of Parliament was necessary in 1779. It ended the £30 loans to contributors. It also made other changes. One was that some vacant stipend became payable. By the law of Ann, the half year's stipend current at the death of the minister, the annat, was payable to the widow. The succeeding minister obtained the right of the benefice from the term of Whitsunday or Michaelmas preceding his admission, except during the currency of the annat. When there was a prolonged vacancy, any stipend to which the previous minister, his widow or the new minister had no claim was known as vacant stipend. A half rate was payable out of the annat, or if no annat, by the heir of the deceased contributor. A half rate, fixed at an average of £3.2.0 was also payable out of each half year's vacant stipend. The object of providing for these payments was to ensure no interruption in the estimated accumulation of the Fund.

The trustees were authorised to raise the capital of the Fund to £100,000 and to lend any part of capital not required, provided they have the consent of three judges of the Courts of Session and Exchequer.

In 1798 the capital of the Fund reached the maximum required of £100,000 and in 1800 the trustees made the first distribution of surplus in proportion to annuities. This practice of giving fluctuating additions continued until 1814. In 1813 Dr Francis Nicoll, a minister in the Dundee district and an ex-moderator, had presented an overture to Assembly on the inadequate level of annuity. The amending Act of 1814 was the result and greatly increased the income of the Fund not only by increasing rates from members, but by bringing in additional sources such as vacant stipends and bishops' rents. Also, prior to the Act, the contributors had entered into a voluntary subscription to augment the new fund and the Act imposed entry money of £10 on future entrants, an amount equivalent to the average subscription.

Most important was the creation of a New Fund to hold all surpluses from which increases in payments would come. Disbursements from the New Fund were to be made in 1815, 1821, 1827 and then only after successive periods of not less than fourteen years. The way in which surplus was to be disposed of was unusual. Only two-thirds of the interest on the surplus plus an average of the income from vacant stipends and other funds was to be distributed by increasing annuities in payment by equal amounts irrespective of class. The trustees are cautioned that "care being always had not to circumscribe too much the operation of the said capital— it being the true meaning and intent of this Act that there shall always belong to such capital such a sum or revenue as may admit, from time to time, of an advance to the annuities of the widows and orphan families, in some degree corres- ponding to what may be the increased expense of living, and to consequent exigencies of their situation." Between 1827 and 1841 the rate of interest obtained on heritable loans had fallen to 3½% and, largely as a result, there was a small deficiency in several years. The trustees were, therefore, unable to make any further increase in annuities in 1841. The fixed additions to date were as follows:

	Original Annuity	Addition 1815	Addition 1821	Addition 1827	Total Annuity
	£	£	£	£	£
1st Class	10	4	2	6	22
2nd Class	15	5	4	6	30
3rd Class	20	7	5	6	38
4th Class	25	8	7	6	46

It may be noted that if the additions in 1815 and 1821 are added together the totals are proportionate to the original annuities, but from 1827 additions were the same for all classes. This change may have been prompted by the fact that a substantial part of the surplus no longer emanated from the ministers' own contributions.

The Ministers' Widows' Fund was particularly suited to establishment as a perpetual fund and the maximum principle worked well for the first hundred years. The number of parishes remained constant and ministers formed a fairly homogeneous population with similar lifestyle and habits and so could be expected to experience common rates of mortality, marriage and issue. In an earlier chapter Scott and Hare have shown how the initial calculations were made leading up to the establishment of the Fund. In his report of 1849, Thomson records how the estimates based on a population of 897 parish ministers were increased proportionately to allow for the inclusion of 65 ministers in universities and then, being considered insufficient "grounds of a scheme for perpetuity" and in consequence of certain calculations based on Halley's Table, were further increased. The following table shows the actual averages experienced in the years 1800–1843, by which time the population might be assumed to have reached a stationary position, compared with the final assumptions originally made.

	Original Expectation	Actual Experience
Number of Contributors	962	1021
Number of Widows	334	337.60
Yearly deaths of Contributors	30	29.84
leaving Widows	20	16.93
leaving only Children	6	6.52
leaving neither	4	6.39

The difference in the number of contributors may even be accounted for by the survivors of those who resigned or were deposed after 1778, since the Act of that date required them to continue in membership and their number averaged just over one per year in this period. The figures illustrate the remarkable skill of the promoters of the Scheme.

In 1831 James Cleghorn, who then described himself as "Accountant" but later was to be one of the first actuaries, completed an actuarial report, the last before the Disruption. The question asked of him was, "What sum would be required to make up the reversion of ten years' annuities to children of those widows who have died before drawing that sum?" His very detailed work led to the conclusion that the funds of the Scheme were very fully committed and that either considerable changes would be required in the Scheme or, he hinted, some other step would require to be taken to deal with the needs of certain families. This led to the creation of the Supplementary Orphan Fund (see Appendix II). The question arose from the practice of not paying any benefit to children over the age of sixteen where the widow died before becoming an annuitant, which could be up to 11 months after the death of the contributor.

In 1836 another problem had to be faced. What was to happen about a new group of ministers? The ministers of Parliamentary churches (designed by Telford, about 1827, in the Highlands, at government cost) wished to come into the Fund. The Court of Session had ruled that "as from the date of induction and at a date fixed by statute, those who have not duly declared their acceptance of one of the rates—are to be charged with interest on the arrears of such rates in terms of the Act." After the Disruption in 1843 the Free Church formed its own Widows' and Orphans' Scheme to provide for ministers who were not members of the Church of Scotland Scheme (see Chapter 5 part (a)).

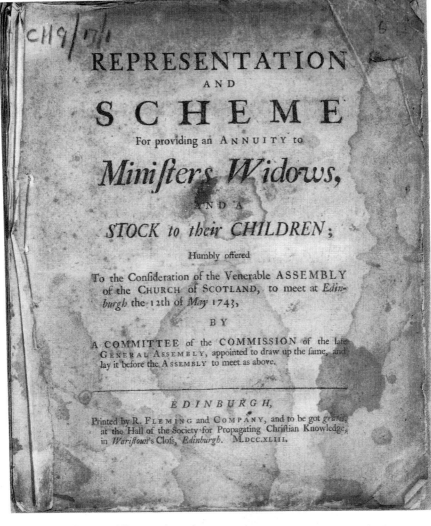

REPRESENTATION
AND
SCHEME

For providing an ANNUITY to

Miniſters Widows,

AND A

STOCK to their CHILDREN;

Humbly offered

To the Conſideration of the Venerable ASSEMBLY
of the CHURCH of SCOTLAND, to meet at *Edinburgh* the 12th of *May* 1743,

BY

A COMMITTEE of the COMMISSION of the late
GENERAL ASSEMBLY, appointed to draw up the ſame, and
lay it before the ASSEMBLY to meet as above.

EDINBURGH,

Printed by R. FLEMING and COMPANY, and to be got *gratis*
at the Hall of the Society for Propagating Chriſtian Knowledge,
in *Wariſton's* Cloſs, *Edinburgh.* M.DCC.XLIII.

1 Scheme for providing an Annuity.
This is the title page of a pamphlet describing the Scheme for
consideration by the General Assembly 12th May 1743.

2 **The Widows' Scheme.**
Part of Colin Maclaurin's calculations of 23rd May 1743—the first actuarially-correct continuing fund calculations in the world (*Scottish Record Office CC 9/17/16/3*).

CALCULATIONS,

WITH THE

PRINCIPLES and DATA

On which they are instituted :

Relative to a late Act of Parliament,

INTITULED,

An Act for raising and establishing a Fund for a Provision for the Widows and Children of the Ministers of the CHURCH, and of the Heads, Principals, and Masters of the Universities of SCOTLAND.

SHEWING

The Rise and Progress of the FUND.

Published by Order of the TRUSTEES nominated in the said Act of Parliament.

EDINBURGH:
Printed by THOMAS LUMISDEN and COMPANY, and sold at their Printing-house in the *Fish-market*, and by the Booksellers in Town. M.DCC.XLVIII.

3 *Calculations with Principles and Data ...*
The title page of the first "Actuarial Report" ever published (1748)
(*Scottish Record Office CH9/17/34/2*).

IT is here proper to insert Mr. *Edmund Halley's* Table so often referred to, traced from the Tables of Births and Funerals in *Breslaw*, the Capital City of *Silesia*, drawn up by Doctor *Newman* of that City, to be found in *Lewthrop's* Abridgment of the *Philosophical Transactions*, 3d Edition, Vol. 3d. Pag. 669.——*Breslaw* is so situated, that the Degrees of Mortality, in that City, seem most proper for a Standard; and therefore the following Table is generally thought to give a more just Idea of the State and Condition of Mankind; than any Thing yet extant.

Mr. HALLEY's TABLE

OF THE

PERSONS that are living, and die yearly, in *Breslaw*, in the several AGES, as under,

	2	3		1	2	3		1.	2.	3.		1.	2.	3			Total.	
Age.	Persons.			Age.	Persons.			Age.	Persons.			Age.	Persons.			Age.	Persons.	
Cur.	Alive.	Dead.		Cur.	Alive.	Dead.		Cur.	Alive.	Dead.		Cur.	Alive.	Dead.		Cur.	Alive.	Deaţ.
1	1000	8		8	680	12		15	628	6		22	586	6		7	5547	308

Age	Persons	Dec.	Age	Persons	Dec.	Age	Persons	Dec.	Age	Persons	Dec.
5	732	28	12	646	7	19	604	6	26	560	7
6	710	22	13	640	6	20	598	6	27	553	7
7	692	18	14	634	6	21	592	6	28	546	7
29	539	7	36	481	9	43	417	10	50	346	11
30	531	8	37	472	9	44	407	10	51	335	11
31	523	8	38	463	9	45	397	10	52	324	11
32	515	8	39	454	9	46	387	10	53	313	11
33	507	8	40	445	9	47	377	10	54	302	11
34	499	8	41	436	9	48	367	10	55	292	10
35	490	9	42	427	9	49	357	10	56	282	10
57	272	10	64	202	10	71	131	11	78	58	10
58	262	10	65	192	10	72	120	11	79	49	9
59	252	10	66	182	10	73	109	11	80	41	8
60	242	10	67	172	10	74	98	11	81	34	7
61	232	10	68	162	10	75	88	10	82	28	6
62	222	10	69	152	10	76	78	10	83	23	5
63	212	10	70	142	10	77	68	10	84	20	3

Summary:

Age	Sum	
21	4270	44
28	3964	46
35	3604	56
42	3178	63
49	2709	70
56	2194	75
63	1694	70
70	1204	70
77	692	74
84	253	48
100	107	20
	34000	1000

4 Mr Halley's Table.

Edmund Halley's famous life table (1693) as it appears in *Calculations with Principles and Data* ... (see Illustration 3) (*Scottish Record Office* CH9/17/342).

Portrait of the Revd Alexander Webster DD by *Daniel Martin*.
Formerly in possession of the Trustees.

The Revd Robert Wallace.
Portrait in possession of the Trustees.

Picture of Colin Maclaurin MA engraved by *S Freeman* from a model by *Percey.*
Reproduced by permission of Edinburgh University Library (EUL Ms DC.2.57).

DISRUPTION TO
AMALGAMATION
1843 - 1930

CHAPTER 5

The Free Church of Scotland and United Presbyterian Church Schemes

The Late William J Cameron MA BD

(a) *The Free Church of Scotland Widows' and Orphans' Fund*

In 1843, when the Fund for the benefit of the Widows and Orphans of the Ministers of the Church and Professors of the Universities of Scotland had been in existence for almost a century, there took place the Disruption in the Church of Scotland and the formation of the Free Church of Scotland. According to J H S Burleigh, the number of ministers who remained in the Church of Scotland was 752 (*A Church History of Scotland*, p. 352). But 451 ministers signed a deed of demission whereby they voluntarily relinquished all the emoluments and privileges to which they had been entitled as ministers of the Church of Scotland, but expressly stated that they were "reserving always the rights and benefits accruing to them, or any of them, under the provisions of the statutes respecting the Ministers' Widows' Fund." The separating ministers still retained their rights in the old Widows' Fund, and were required by the governing Act of Parliament to continue contributing. It was in their interests to do so, and subsequent Free Church provision excepted them from the new provision that was made. However, new ministers were not eligible to join the old fund, and notwithstanding the gigantic task confronting the Free Church in providing church buildings, manses, schools, a theological college and funds for the maintenance of their ministers, provision of a fund yielding comparable benefits to the widows and orphans of Free Church ministers was accorded a high priority.

As early as 1844, the Free Church General Assembly appointed a committee to consider how to provide a Widows' and Orphans' Fund and report to the Commission of Assembly at any of its diets, or to next General Assembly. If mention of the Commission implies a sense of urgency, the desire to make a thorough investigation of possible methods probably prevented the presentation of the Report before the following Assembly. The Convener then disclosed that the committee had received many suggestions and offers of help in establishing a Widows' Fund. Specially valuable advice came from Mr Findlayson, a government actuary in London, but after due deliberation the committee chose to be guided by Mr Low, "a very experienced actuary in Edinburgh", because it was easy to be in regular communication with him. Six hundred and twenty-seven circulars were issued to ministers, of which 613 were returned giving the required data. From these Mr Low prepared statistical tables and made the necessary calculations, which were checked by Mr Griffith Davies, the actuary of a similar fund established for the benefit of Army Officers' Widows in India. Mr Low's proposals were as follows.

Contributions to the Widows' Fund should be compulsory at the rate of £5 payable on the 25th day of May annually. Entry money should be £10 payable in two years, i.e. every member should pay double rates for the first two years. A marriage-tax of £5 should be payable on 25th May after marriage by all aged below 45, and for all aged above 45 such tax should be £10, whereof £5 should be payable as above and the remainder on 25th May following. There should be a separate contribution of £2 per annum to form a distinct fund, to be called the Orphans' Fund for the benefit of the bereaved children of contributors, each child to receive an annuity till the age of eighteen years. The Funds would be for the benefit of ministers and professors who were not contributors to the old established Widows' Fund. Mr Low anticipated that the Fund proposed would yield annually for each widow £27 and for each child £10, to commence at the father's death, to be increased to £15 on the death of the surviving parent, but to cease on the child attaining the age of 18. The Report pointed out that under the proposed Scheme a widow with five children would be entitled to receive £50 on their behalf, whereas the maximum amount available to her under the old established Scheme for widows and orphans of ministers was £46.

The General Assembly approved of the Scheme and embodied it in Act XVI of 1845 Assembly, which Act required that the necessary contributions be paid regularly out of the dividends due to the several members from the Free Church Sustentation Fund. The Act also appointed a committee, consisting of the Presbyteries of Glasgow and Edinburgh, with powers to frame rules and regulations of whatever kind they considered necessary to carry the Report into full effect, and to appoint a sub-committee of management. The following year the General Assembly considered the Constitution, Rules and Regulations submitted to them, approved of them and incorporated them in Act III, 1846. The regulations which numbered 27 included a paragraph to the effect that:

"Those ministers and professors of the said church (i.e. of the Free Church of Scotland) who are contributors to the Widows' Fund of the Established Church of Scotland and their widows and children are exempt from the Fund hereby established, and no payment shall be made in respect of such ministers and professors, or the congregations or chairs of which they are or shall be the incumbents for the time being respectively, nor shall any claim be competent under either of the said schemes on behalf of the widows and children of such ministers and professors."

Two sections related to the obligation of Presbytery Clerks and individual ministers and professors to make such returns to the Clerk of the Fund as would enable him to keep "a full and correct record to the statistics of the Fund."

Each Presbytery Clerk was required at his admission to office to affirm his obligation to pay a penalty of £5 for each omission to make timeous report of all changes that took place within the bounds of his Presbytery. Every minister or professor failing to make a return in the month of August each year, giving an account of such changes as had taken place in his family during the preceding year, or certifying that no change had taken place, would forfeit his right to the stipend or dividend that would have been payable to him at the ensuing term, which right would revive only on his making the requisite return. And to the intent that this rule be duly enforced, the Clerk of the Fund was instructed to furnish, on or before 5th of November in each year, a list of defaulting ministers and professors to the treasurer of the Sustentation Fund or College Fund, who thereupon was required to withhold the payment of the stipend or dividend that otherwise would have been due to such parties respectively, until he received intimation from the Clerk of the Fund that the necessary returns had been made.

These regulations show that those who framed them anticipated the possibility of the same kind of hindrance to the working of the scheme as was met with by the trustees of the old established Fund a century earlier. In 1745 the said trustees had complained to the General Assembly of the Church of Scotland that it was only with the greatest difficulty they could instruct their collector in due time because of the failure of Presbyteries to make timeous returns.

The Free Church Scheme established by Act of Assembly in 1846 remained in force for five years. At the end of that period the number of members had risen to 528, but it was believed that the Scheme might be more efficiently and beneficially operated if it were established by Act of Parliament. Accordingly appropriate steps were taken and in 1851 an Act of Parliament was passed called "The Free Church Ministers' Widows' and Orphans' Fund Act", the preamble of which was in the following terms:

"Whereas a general fund is annually contributed by the congregations of the body of Christians calling themselves the Free Church of Scotland, for the support of the ministers of the said Church, which fund is commonly called and known by the name of the Sustentation Fund, and another general fund is annually contributed by the congregations of the said church for the support of Professors holding professors' offices in any college connected with the said Church, which fund is commonly called and known by the name of the College Fund: And whereas the General Assembly of the said Church did, in terms of an Act of Assembly, dated the twenty-seventh day of May one thousand eight hundred and forty-six, form a scheme for raising out of the general fund called the Sustentation Fund and out of the said general fund called the College Fund, a fund for the purpose of making provision for the widows and children of the ministers of the said church and for the widows and children of professors holding professors' offices in any college connected with the said church: and whereas a considerable sum has already been accumulated in pursuance of the scheme for the purpose aforesaid: And whereas experience has shown that the said scheme and the administration thereof may be improved and its objects more beneficially effected, but this cannot be done without the aid and authority of Parliament" [it was enacted as follows:]

"That there shall be raised and established a fund for making a provision for the widows and children of the said church and of professors holding professors' offices in any college in Scotland connected with the said church, and with which the fund already raised shall be united and amalgamated, and which amalgamated fund shall be called the Free Church Ministers' Widows' and Orphans' Fund."

The subsequent sections of the Act embody with little variation the regulations of Act III, 1846 of the Free Church General Assembly, and include the paragraph exempting from the scheme ministers and professors who contributed to the Widows' Fund of the Established Church of Scotland.

The next significant event in the history of the Free Church Widows' and Orphans' Fund resulted from the union effected in 1876 between the Free Church of Scotland and the Reformed Presbyterian Church of Scotland. Act X of the Free Church Assembly of that year makes reference to the admission of the Reformed Presbyterian ministers to the benefits of the Free Church Widows' and Orphans' Fund as underwritten:

"They [the General Assembly] also sanction the agreement between the Committees of both Churches as to the raising of the Capital required to render equitable the admission of the Reformed Presbyterian ministers to the benefits of the Free Church Widows' and Orphans' Fund. The General Assembly remit to the Commission in August to take such steps as may be necessary to complete the arrangements."

Thirty-seven additional ministers were consequently added to the membership of the Fund in 1877, which brought the total number of additions for that year to 61 as compared with 27 in the previous year, making the entire number of members at the end of that year 1067.[1]

In 1888, the 1851 Act of Parliament was amended by a new Act of Parliament known as The Free Church of Scotland Ministers' and Missionaries' Widows' and Orphans' Fund Act. By this Act, separate Funds raised by the Free Church of Scotland's Foreign Missions Committee, Continental Committee, Colonial Committee and Jewish Conversion Committee respectively for the benefit of the Widows and Orphans of Missionaries under the superintendance of each Committee, were amalgamated with the Fund established under the provisions of the Free Church Ministers' Widows' and Orphans' Act 1851, so as to form a common Fund to be managed by the trustees appointed and incorporated by the said Act 1851. Section IX of the 1888 Act provided that the above noted provision for Widows and Orphans of Missionaries of the said Church be subject to special climatic rates and to a medical examination of the missionary before he leaves this country. As a result of the admission of missionaries to the Fund, 61 new members were added in 1888 bringing the total membership at the end of that year to 1288. Twelve years later in 1900 membership had risen to 1402.[2] In that year the majority of the Free Church of Scotland united with the United Presbyterian Church of Scotland to form the United Free Church of Scotland, leaving a small minority who retained the name and constitution of the Free Church and successfully laid claim to the whole property formerly held by the Free Church. In

1905 an Act of Parliament[3] appointed Commissioners to allocate between the Free Church of Scotland and the United Free Church of Scotland

> "All the property which on thirtieth October nineteen hundred was vested in or held by, or on trust for or was payable to or behoof the Free Church ... and to make such orders as they may consider necessary for carrying into effect any allocation under this Act including modification of the Acts relating to the Widows' and Orphans' Fund."

Order 19 of the said Commission states that

> "Whereas the said Widows' and Orphans' Fund is included in the property which by the said Act and Commission are authorised to allocate"—[here follows a narrative of the history of the fund from 1846, concluding with the following sections]—"and whereas application has been made to the Commission for an allocation of the interests of the said Churches in the said Fund by giving effect to a scheme whereby widows and orphans of ministers, professors and missionaries of both Churches shall be entitled to the benefits of the Fund, which necessitates various modifications in the said Acts, and the Commission have resolved after inquiring into the circumstances, to give effect to the scheme, therefore the Commissioners acting under the Church (Scotland) Act 1905 and by virtue of the powers conferred on them by that Act hereby order as follows:
> "The Order may be called The Free Church (Scotland) Widows and Orphans Fund Order, 1907 ..."

Sections 4 and 5 deal with the payment to be made by the United Free Church of Scotland and directed that

> "In respect that each of the ministers, professors and missionaries admitted to the benefit of the Fund is estimated to bring in average a loss upon the Fund, the contributions not being sufficient to provide the present benefits, the

United Free Church of Scotland shall pay into the Fund as at the commencement of this Order such capital sum as in the opinion of Mr Neil Ballingal Gunn, F.F.A., shall fairly represent the estimated amount of the additional obligations entailed upon the Fund in consequence of the average annual number of ministers, professors and missionaries who subsequent to thirtieth October 1900 shall under the provisions of this Order be admitted to the Fund, being increased by admission of charges which were formerly connected with the United Presbyterian Church, and in consequence of the translation of ministers of the United Presbyterian Church to charges of the United Free Church of Scotland, with interest on such capital sum at the rate of three per cent from the commencement of this Order, until payment. Provided always that there shall be taken into account the annual payments to be made to the Fund in terms of this Order and the dates at which such payments commence, and there shall be taken into account the possibility of the number of congregations in the United Free Church of Scotland being in future reduced by the amalgamation of congregations formerly of the United Presbyterian Church with congregations formerly of the Free Church of Scotland."

Paragraph 47 provides that it shall be in the power of the trustees as they see fit to make arrangements on such terms as may be mutually agreed for taking over the property of the Society known as the United Presbyterian Ministers' Friendly Society. It shall be competent for the trustees on obtaining an actuarial report showing the surplus value of the Society over its liabilities to pay to the United Free Church of Scotland a sum equivalent to such surplus value in consideration of the payment to be made to the Fund by the United Free Church of Scotland in terms of section four hereof.

The Order brought to an end the existence of two separate schemes, one for Widows and one for Children respectively, and stated that the Fund raised and established under the former Acts and this Order shall be constituted in one scheme for the widows and children of ministers, of the said

Churches, and the professors holding office in any Colleges in Scotland connected with the said Churches. There were excepted from the benefits of the Fund as established by the Order all ministers, professors and missionaries who were prior to 30h October, 1900 ministers, professors and missionaries of the United Presbyterian Church and who subsequent to that date shall have remained or shall remain ministers, professors or missionaries holding in the United Church of Scotland which prior to the said date were charges in the United Presbyterian Church, until such time as they may be transferred to charges which prior to that date were Free Church charges or new charges in the United Free Church created subsequently to that date.

No further major change took place in the constitution of the Fund until the Union of the United Free Church with the Church of Scotland in 1929.

(b) *The United Presbyterian Ministers' Friendly Society*

The United Presbyterian Ministers' Friendly Society, already referred to, was formed by the union of the Friendly Society of Ministers in connection with the Relief Synod and the Friendly Society of Dissenting Ministers in Scotland. Of these the earlier was that connected with the Relief Synod. It originated from resolutions adopted by the Synod in May 1791, which formed the basis of its constitution. An overture had come before the Synod in 1775 regarding a proposal to provide a Fund for the benefit of ministers' widows and orphans. A Scheme, devised at that time, was sent to congregations, requiring a collection to be made at the following Martinmas and a committee to meet during that term to grant discharges of the sums collected. Every member who adopted the scheme was required to pay an annual sum at the rate of £2, and entrants to the ministry were to be subject to the same rate of £2 immediately after ordination. Thus the Funds of the Scheme were derived from minister members and congregations. For the first four years no widow was to receive more than £20 per annum, but it was reckoned that thereafter the sum could be increased to £30.

The Scheme did not fare well because congregations failed to make regular collections and it was found that some ministers could not afford to pay £2. To improve matters the 1785 Synod reduced the annual rate payable by ministers to £1.10s. The Synod also required each member, whether minister or probationer, to enter the Scheme and subscribe a bond to maintain payments at the new rate. Each widow was to receive £12 per annum. In the event of the death of both parents the minister's children would receive £12 per annum until the age of 15 years. This became more or less the Scheme approved in 1791. The Society remained closely connected with the Synod. The treasurer's accounts were included in those of the Synod treasurer and both offices were frequently held by the same person. A collection was taken for the Society at the opening of the Synod and the annual meeting was called from the Moderator's chair. In 1819 the Society's income was £445.10.4½, annuities to widows amounted to £110 and expenses of management were £7.0.9½. The first mention of an actuarial investigation into the financial condition of the Society occurs in 1838 when a proposal to change rates from guineas to pounds came before the Society which resolved at that time to make no change in payments.

In 1847, the year of the union between the Relief and the Secession Churches, the income of the Society from rates, collections and interest totalled £714.7.9 and the capital amounted to £7551.14.1. Following upon the Union, consideration was given to the future of the Society. Three proposals were discussed: (a) to close the Society, (b) to arrange for amalgamation with some similar Society, (c) to enlarge its basis and to admit entrants from new quarters. The last of these found most favour and prior to considering it further an actuarial investigation was entrusted to a Mr Borland who reported a surplus of £1521.14.7 in favour of the Society, which was steadily augmenting. At the 1848 annual meeting it was unanimously agreed to throw open the Society for admission of members of the United Presbyterian Church on the usual terms. Also two medical officers were appointed from whom all future applicants were required to obtain a certificate of health. The treasurer's salary was fixed at £20 per annum. Premiums were to be graduated according to age, and the annual meeting was no longer to be called from the Moderator's Chair, but by a circular sent to every member of the Society.

In 1851 the Society resolved to conform with the requirements of the Friendly Societies' Act and accordingly appointed an actuarial investigation for the beginning and middle of every decade. At the same time the practice of collecting rates in Presbyteries by sub-treasurers was abolished. From 1852 the name of the Society was altered to "The Friendly Society of Ministers in connection with the United Presbyterian Church" for providing annuities for their widows and orphans. Five years later the following adjustments were made in the regulations. The age to which orphans were entitled to benefit was extended from 15 to 18. The number of payments necessary before a widow would receive benefit was reduced from 18 to 12. Premiums ceased to be payable by entrants and the treasurer was required to deduct income tax from payments to beneficiaries and to inform them as to how they might recover it from the government. On the recommendation of the actuary in 1860, the Society agreed to apply the surplus to increase by one-sixth the annuities of widows and orphans, and to increase them by one-twelfth for the following five years. Subsequent increases granted after quinquennial investigations indicated the increasing prosperity of the Fund. By 1882 members were released from making further payments on attaining the age of 65 and having made 35 payments without arrears. At the same time the treasurer's salary was increased to £40.

In 1888 the Society began consultations with the Friendly Society of Dissenting Ministers in Scotland as to the possibility of amalgamation, and in 1892 agreement was reached that the two Societies become amalgamated as one Society to be known as The United Presbyterian Ministers' Friendly Society and that upon the undernoted terms:

1. That the rules of the United Presbyterian Ministers' Friendly Society formed by the amalgamation of the Friendly Society of Ministers in connection with the United Presbyterian Church for providing annuities for their

widows and orphans, instituted 1792, with the Friendly Society of Dissenting Ministers in Scotland, instituted at Edinburgh 20th June 1797, conform to the special resolutions of the said Societies passed on 15th February 1892, confirmed on 1st March 1892 and 31st March 1892 respectively and assented to by the members of the said societies respectively, all in terms of the Friendly Societies' Acts, submitted to this meeting in draft, a copy of which is signed by the chairman of this meeting as relative hereto, shall be the rules of the amalgamated Society, with power to the directors to make such modifications as they find necessary or convenient for carrying the same into effect.

2.   That the whole assets of the Society, and the whole assets of the Friendly Society of Dissenting Ministers, shall be transferred and made over to the said amalgamated Society, which shall become liable to pay and implement the whole debts and obligations of the Society and the said Friendly Society of Dissenting Ministers in Scotland.

3.   That the name of the Society be changed to The United Presbyterian Ministers' Friendly Society.

At the time of amalgamation the Funds of the Relief Society amounted to £36,968.16.1 and the total sum possessed by the new Society at the outset was £60,334.12.2. The sum raised by annual rates àmounted to £2184.5.11 and interest on investments was £2498.3.9. The treasurer's salary was fixed at £60 and that of the secretary at £30. It was resolved to admit all ministerial members of the Synod who chose to apply, on payments to be calculated by the actuary. Also all missionaries then appointed were required to join the Society, on payment of the same rates and entry money when due, the Foreign Board paying £2 per annum of extra rates. Licentiates ordained for the discharge of pastoral functions but without ordination to a special charge were not to be eligible for membership. In 1894 the treasurer's salary was raised to £100 per annum.

In 1900 the annual meeting remitted to the Directors to consider the effect of the contemplated union with the

Free Church with reference to future admission of United Presbyterian ministers. As a result the following resolution was adopted:

"That all ministers of congregations of the United Free Church of Scotland which before the union on 31st October 1900 were congregations of the United Presbyterian Church and all missionaries from the home church, ordained or medical, in foreign mission stations which before the union were stations of the United Presbyterian Church, shall be eligible for membership, subject to the following conditions:- Ministers shall be admitted only if they apply within one year from ordination, and missionaries only if they apply within one year from the date of their appointment by the Foreign Mission Committee."

During the years between 1900 and the issuing of the Commissioners' Ordinance regarding the allocation of the Funds of the Free Church of Scotland, the Funds of the Society steadily increased. The Ordinance issued in 1907 contained a clause to the effect that all ministers admitted to charges in the former United Presbyterian Church after 1900 should become members of the Free Church Widows' and Orphans' Fund, but absolutely shutting out all ministers ordained in the United Presbyterian Church before the said date. To meet this provision the Society passed the under-noted resolution in 1908:

"Any member who shall withdraw from the Society on his admission to the Free Church (of Scotland) Widows' and Orphans' Fund shall be entitled to receive payment without interest of the marriage rate which may have been paid by him to the Society in respect of a marriage existing at the time of his withdrawal, provided that intimation is made to the treasurer or secretary within six months from the date of such admission, or from the date of the registration of this rule, whichever shall later happen. And if such member shall have been ordained after 31st October 1900 and shall intimate his withdrawal before 3rd April, 1909 he shall be entitled to receive repayment without interest of the marriage rate which may have been paid by him to the Society in respect of a marriage at the time of his withdrawal, and shall also be entitled to receive repayment without interest of the annual rates due on 25th June 1907 and 20th June 1908 if the same have been paid by him. Any member so withdrawing shall upon intimation of his withdrawal, cease to be a member of the Society and have no claim for the money which has been paid to it, except as above provided for, and shall forfeit all privileges what so ever arising from the Society. The directors shall have no power to repone any member who has so withdrawn or to restore him to the privileges of the Society."

Because of surplus money disclosed at the 1907 quinquennial investigation the Society was able, on and after January 1909, to make a 10% addition to the annuities paid to beneficiaries, and in certain cases, where the full annuity could not be paid on account of the maximum specified by the Friendly Societies Act, the Society agreed that a separate benefit of equivalent value be paid. In 1910 the treasurer's salary was increased to £120 and that of the secretary to £50.

At the time of the 1900 Union, Mr Gunn, the actuary appointed by the Free Church, reported that if ministers ordained to congregations of the former United Presbyterian Church were admitted to membership of the Free Church Widows' and Orphans' Fund, a capital sum varying from £20,000 to £23,000 would require to be added to the Fund, to meet which necessity sums amounting to £13,000 or £15,000 were available from the funds of the United Presbyterian Church. He also threw out the suggestion that the estimated surplus of the Friendly Society, calculated by him as £9914, might be applied to meet the debt due to the United Free Church Widows' and Orphans' Fund. The proposal was communicated to the secretary of the Society but remained in abeyance until 1911, when the Finance Committee of the United Free Church approached the Directors asking whether they could not see their way to allocate £6000 from their surplus Fund to reduce the debt to the Free Church Widows' and Orphans' Fund. The memorandum which embodied the request referred to the clause in the Commissioners' Ordinance regarding the possibility of union between the Friendly Society and the Widows' and Orphans' Fund. In 1915 the Society came to the following findings with regard to the 1911 communication:

"This meeting concurs in the opinion of the Directors that the whole resources of the Society must be reserved for the purpose of increasing the benefits of its own annuitants and therefore declines to entertain the proposal of the (Free Church) Finance Committee."

Correspondence was exchanged and a meeting with representatives of the said Finance Committee was arranged, and not until 1916 did the Society intimate its final decision which was in these terms:

"The Society approves and adopts the notes of the Directors regarding the Finance Committee's application, again reaffirms its former decision, adheres to its resolve to retain independent control of its own affairs under the Friendly Societies Act, and itself administer its funds for behoof of its own beneficiaries present and presumptive, and declines to continue further discussion of the subject."

Meanwhile a surplus of £15,127 had been reported at the 1912 investigation and this had been applied to extend several benefits which were granted to widows and orphans of the old United Presbyterian ministers prior to the amalgamation in 1892. When a minister died leaving no widow but unmarried daughters, or an unmarried daughter, these would receive for ten years the amount that would have been paid to his widow. The rule by which ministers of the United Presbyterian Church ceased payment of annual rates at sixty-five years of age was extended to include all members of the Society. Annuities payable to all widows and orphans of former members of the Friendly Society of

Ministers connected with the United Presbyterian Church were increased by 10%.

Further increases were made, in all the annuities payable, in 1917. The actuary found that the number of members on the roll of the Society was 259 and the accumulated funds amounted to £98,191.18.6. Detailed information beyond this date is not available. It is noteworthy that the Funds of the Society were wholly raised by the ministers themselves without external aid apart from a few legacies left by ministers or ministers' widows. Management expenses all along were small in proportion to the business of the Society. A report in 1919 showed that after nearly 120 years it was still in a most flourishing condition and able to continue its good work among ministers of the former United Presbyterian Church.

Rev James Jeffrey, DD, to whose history of the Society the foregoing narrative and statistical information is largely indebted, wrote toward the close of his account in 1919[4]:

> "It is not for me to say what the future of the Society may be. It is bound to work itself out in time, but not before the benefits to widows at least be raised to the same level as those of the Free Church (Scotland) Widows' and Orphans' Fund. When that time comes it will be for the surviving members of the Society to determine what shall be done with the surplus, if any, that remains."

Doubtless in the intervening period between then and now, there came a time when the Society ceased to exist, but the circumstances in which that took place have not yet been ascertained.

Mention of the Society ceased to appear in the *Church of Scotland Year-Book* in 1965.

(c) *The Friendly Society of Dissenting Ministers of Scotland instituted 20th June 1797*

The purpose of the Society was to establish permanently a fund for granting annuities to widows and orphans of ministers. In course of time membership was opened to ministers of the Gospel without respect of denomination. The regulations were kept in constant review so as to ensure that they conformed to the requirements of successive Acts of Parliament relating to Friendly Societies from 1829 onwards. The following[5] are dated 1861 when the actuary reporting in terms of statute was Mr James Watson:

Entry: Ministers must apply before the expiry of one year from the date of ordination. Each applicant must furnish in writing his date of birth and if married the date of his wife's birth, and also a medical certificate regarding the state of his health.

Classes: The Society shall consist of five classes and each person must indicate the class of his choice. He may afterwards take a lower but not a higher class. No part of the sums paid by him may be returned and the widow's benefit is to be determined by the class he chooses.

Entry money and age tax: and the amount of annual rate less age tax payable by those in each class are indicated below:

	Class I	*Class II*	*Class III*	*Class IV*	*Class V*
	£1.8.0	£2.2.0	£2.16.0	£3.10.0	£4.4.0
Age tax	7.0	10.6	14.0	17.6	£1.1.0
Annual Rate	£1.8.0	£2.2.0	£2.16.0	£3.10.0	£4.4.0

Age tax which was not exigible until the second year was to be calculated at the above rates for every year the entrant exceeded twenty-five years of age. Fines for late payment of annual rates were to be imposed at the rate of four to twelve pence for each month, according to class, until payment was made, but if two years elapsed since the date of initial arrears all claims to refunds or benefit would be forfeited.

Redemption and commutation: It shall be permissible to redeem annual rates by payment of a single lump sum, or to commute them into an increased payment, to cease on a member's completion of his sixtieth or sixty-fifth year.

Payment of Widows' Annuities: A widow's annuity shall not be payable unless full payment of annual rates has been made by her husband but if a husband be deceased, his widow or her friends may pay up arrears in his payment, but after such payment she shall be entitled to only half of the annuity until deduction of the other half and the annual rates (exclusive of entry money, etc.) shall amount to a sum of three full annuities of the class to which her husband belonged. If, however, instead of this annual deduction she or her friends at any time shall pay up the full balance, the full amount of the annuity shall be payable to her from that date. If a wife shall pre-decease her husband leaving children, the annuity which would have been due to her shall be payable to the children until the youngest has attained the age of sixteen years.

Administration: A President, Vice-president and Clerk shall be elected annually, and three out of ten directors shall go out of office in rotation and be replaced each year. Five persons shall be chosen as arbiters in disputes, three of whom shall be called to deal with each case that may arise, and their decisions shall not be subject to any appeals in the Law Courts.

Mortality Report: The Clerk shall be obliged to transmit to the Registrar of Friendly Societies within three months of 31st December 1865, and thereafter at the end of each five years, a return of the rate of mortality experienced by the Society within the preceding four years.

Actuarial Investigation: The affairs of the Society shall be investigated periodically by a qualified actuary, and his advice shall be taken in regard to any proposals for an increase in the rate of annuities.

References

1   A Hewat: Widows and Pensions Fund, 1902: Appendix 14.
2   H Hewat: op cit. Friendly Society: Appendix 15.
3   5 Ed 7: chapter 12.
4   James Jeffrey: *United Presbyterian Ministers' Friendly Society Historical Sketch,* 1919.
5   cf *Regulations*: instituted 20 June (1797, 1845, 1961)

CHAPTER 6

Notes on the
Church of Scotland Fund
1843-1930

At the time of the Disruption in 1843 the Fund was operated under Act of Parliament 1779 as amended in 1814. About 270 ministers who left to join the Free Church retained their membership of the Fund. The charges vacated by the seceding ministers were soon filled and the membership was thus substantially increased if only on a temporary basis.

An increasing number of quoad sacra charges, the ministers of which were not eligible to join, led to several confusing Court of Session decisions, notably in that of St Margaret's Edinburgh. After an overture from Linlithgow Presbytery in 1886, an Amending Act of Parliament was passed (53 and 54 Vict. cap. 124) to lay down the procedure under which quoad sacra ministers could join.

The first new Act since the 1779 Act, was passed in 1923 (13 and 14 George V Sess. 1923) with the Union of the Churches in 1929 in sight. The 1923 Act made changes in the appointment of trustees. There should be 19—8 from the Presbytery of Edinburgh, 5 from the Synod of Glasgow and Ayr, 1 from the Synod of Aberdeen, 1 from the Synod of Perth and Stirling and 4 appointed by the University of Edinburgh. The 1923 Act was amended in 1926 (16 and 17 George V Sess. 1926). It dealt principally with Vacant Stipend matters.

The Collectors in the period were:

Rev Dr Robert Gordon, Edinburgh St Andrew's (Joined Free Church 1843 but acted until Assembly of 1844)

Rev Dr James Grant, Edinburgh St Mary's 1844–1860 (Resigned)
Henry Cheyne *Esq* WS (after another withdrew over bond of Annuity) 1860–1868 (Died)
Alex. T Niven *Esq* 1869–1878 (Resigned)
Prof John T Maclagan 1879–1897 (Died)
Charles E W MacPherson CA 1897–1930

The Clerks to the Trustees were:

H Maxwell Inglis WS 1831–1879
H Herbert Inglis 1879–1907 (Died)
Fred. P Milligan WS 1908–1930

The Actuaries were:

William Thomas Thomson FFA (Standard Life) Investigations as at 1849, 1861
James Meikle FFA (Scottish Provident) 1875, 1891
Archibald Hewat FFA FIA FSS (Edinburgh Life) 1904
Alexander Fraser FFA FIA FRSE (Edinburgh Life) 1918, 1925 (Also acted for Church of Scotland, with Andrew R. Davidson FFA FIA FSS for Free Church of Scotland, in negotiations for Amalgamation of Funds in 1930).

CHAPTER 7

Actuarial Investigations up to the Amalgamation of the Schemes in 1930

George C Philip FFA

Between 1843 and 1849 there were three important changes which took place in the Church and were to effect the Scheme. These were:

1. The Disruption in 1843 when 270 ministers left the Church but continued in the Scheme and 270 new ministers replaced them and joined the Scheme;
2. The erection by Act of Parliament of 30 new parishes of which 6 were already filled by ministers who had become members of the Scheme; and
3. An increase in the number of ministers who either resigned or were deprived of their benefices. For the first 90 years the number averaged only 1.8 each year, but for the following 11 years the average had risen to 5.8 each year.

In 1848 the Institute of Actuaries had been founded in London and one of its leading Scottish members, William Thomas Thomson, then Manager of the Standard Life Assurance Company, was asked by the trustees in 1849 to report on the effect of these changes on the finances of the Scheme. At this time the records of the Scheme kept by the Collector were only those required to enable contributions to be collected and annuities paid. Individual age and marital status of members were not, therefore, available to the Actuary and this influenced his approach to the problem. In his report he wrote:

"I beg now to bring under notice the result of a calculation which I have made for the purpose of shewing in what time the seceding members will die off and the burden which they bring will be exhausted. In making this calculation I have assumed that those who left the Church were a fair proportion of the whole, old and young, and for the purpose of shewing satisfactorily the value of those burdens from the experience of the Scheme itself, I have traced 992 contributors alive in 1798 down to the present time, following them out individually till 1849, when 16 still remained alive; and the burden which they will create I have further provided for by a calculation proceeding also on the past experience of the Scheme. In this way I have obtained a sufficient groundwork on which to found my estimate of the burdens which the 270 and other resigning members will create, and I have in accordance therewith, fixed the sum requisite to be set apart for that object."

At the same time Thomson calculated the extra capital which had accrued as a result of the Secession, the largest part of which represented vacant stipends, and found that this was not far short of the sum he had calculated as required to support the seceding members. The remaining increase in capital which could be regarded as the true surplus for the period he found insufficient to enable him to recommend any increase in the annuities. In his report he addressed the members in these terms: "Let them rest satisfied in comparing the benefits they enjoy with what they could derive from any other source by a similar expenditure."

As regards the introduction of 270 new ministers to replace those who had seceded, he concluded that as they were likely to be, on average, younger than those who had left, it was his opinion that the Scheme would not suffer by the change. As only 6 ministers from the new parishes, had so far, joined the Scheme, he considered that this question could safely be left for a future date when more would be known.

In view of current legislation requiring account to be

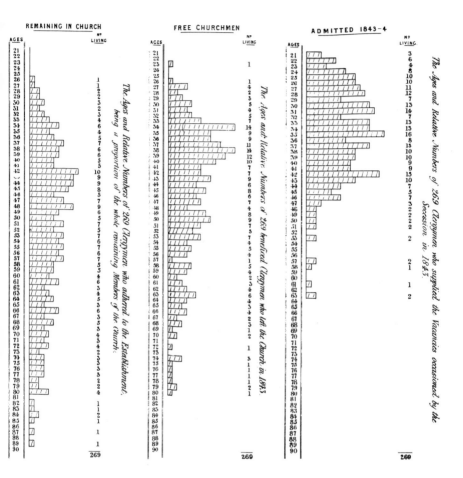

taken of the "reasonable expectation of policyholders", it is interesting to find the trustees, in reporting that no increase in annuities could be afforded, explaining "of the possibility of this they did not themselves entertain any very sanguine hope; but they were aware that a general expectation had been excited among many parties interested in the matter, who were imperfectly acquainted with the circumstances, and who looked chiefly or exclusively to the large accumulation of funds that had of late years taken place."

In 1861 Thomson was again asked to advise whether any additions could be made to the annuities. Up to this time the Fund had been conducted and investigated entirely on a consideration of the Scheme with reference to its maximum condition. For the first 100 years, the Fund fulfilled all the conditions requisite to such a society, but since then the disturbances in the Scheme had altered the situation and made the method more difficult to apply without chance of error. The alternative approach known as the "Individual" system treats each member separately, calculating according to his age and marital status, the liability he brings to the Scheme. In asking the trustees to agree to this change, Thomson quoted the opinion of another actuarial heavy-weight, James Cleghorn, who had reported on the Advocates' Widows' Fund and the Writers to the Signet Widows' Fund and expressed himself thus: "Since the fanciful practice of calculating for a body, indefinite in the number of its members, upon the assumption that the widows will come to a maximum, has been exploded with all intelligent actuaries, there is no other method than to calculate for each individual . . ."

The trustees agreed and schedules were issued to all members requiring them to give full details of themselves and their dependants. Thomson used the information provided by the schedules to test the assumptions made in his previous valuation and to show that changes had occurred in the membership of the Scheme which made the use of the maximum system unreliable. The diagrams on page 106 are an example of the use he made of the schedules to test his previous assumption that those who seceded were a fair proportion of the whole, old and young.

Thomson now submitted an interim report and asked the trustees, "Is it right that I should, with so many disturbing influences at work, be expected to make guesses at truth in the 'maximum' system, while, by the application of calculation founded on the ages now in my possession, I can, by the exercise of the necessary labour and skill, shew the true results in the Fund under the 'individual' system. In short, I must professionally decline to attempt to carry out the 'maximum' system under the existing circumstances of the Fund."

Thomson's final report was a model of what a report should be. In it he explained each assumption made, arguing the case logically and expressing himself in language even the layman could understand. In determining the rate of interest to be used in the valuation, he examined the rates earned over the previous 79 years. The first 39 years he discarded as exceptional, the rates having only varied between 4½ and 5%. During the last 40 years, however, the rates had varied from 3½ to 5% with an average of 3.96%; and from this period he felt "enabled, not only to draw my conclusions authoritatively from the past, but to predicate with confidence for the future." Allowing a small deduction for income tax (the Fund was then taxed on interest less annuities) he assumed a rate of 3½%. As regards mortality he decided to use the Carlisle Tables, and in order to show that they were applicable to this Fund he collected the statistics of life and death among the ministers from 1843 to 1861 and produced the following table:

COMPARATIVE TABLE shewing the Yearly Mortality at each age, according to the Carlisle Mortality Table, and according to the results in the Ministers' Widows' Fund, also the Expectation of Life deduced from these Tables.

Age	Carlisle Table.		Ministers' Widows' Fund.				Expectation of Life		
			Males		Females		Carlisle	Ministers' Fund	
	Living	Dying	Living	Dying	Living	Dying		Males.	Females.
30	5642	57	5748	56	...	...	34.34	36.46	
31	5585	57	5692	17	...	...	33.68	35.81	
32	5528	56	5675	31	...	...	33.03	34.93	
33	5472	55	5644	46	...	...	32.36	34.11	
34	5417	55	5598	...	...	...	31.68	33.38	
35	5362	55	5598	39	...	...	31.00	32.38	
36	5307	56	5559	37	...	...	30.32	31.61	
37	5251	57	5522	58	...	...	29.64	30.82	
38	5194	58	5464	56	...	...	28.96	30.14	
39	5136	61	5408	63	...	...	28.28	29.44	

Continued

Age	Carlisle Table.		Ministers' Widows' Fund.				Expectation of Life		
			Males		Females			Ministers' Fund	
							Carlisle		
	Living	Dying	Living	Dying	Living	Dying		Males.	Females.
40	5075	66	5345	29	...	...	27.61	28.79	
41	5009	69	5316	38	...	...	26.97	27.94	
42	4940	71	5278	18	...	...	26.34	27.14	
43	4869	71	5260	26	...	...	25.71	26.23	
44	4798	71	5234	25	4798	92	25.09	25.35	26.38
45	4727	70	5209	16	4706	90	24.46	24.47	25.89
46	4657	69	5193	71	4616	67	23.82	23.55	25.38
47	4588	67	5122	39	4549	59	23.17	22.86	24.75
48	4521	63	5083	62	4490	...	22.50	22.04	24.07
49	4458	61	5021	46	4490	46	21.81	21.31	23.07
50	4397	59	4975	85	4444	44	21.11	20.50	22.30
51	4338	62	4890	69	4400	90	20.39	19.85	21.52
52	4276	65	4821	77	4310	83	19.68	19.12	20.96
53	4211	68	4744	79	4227	40	18.97	18.42	20.36
54	4143	70	4665	157	4187	38	18.28	17.73	19.55
55	4073	73	4508	128	4149	...	17.58	17.33	18.73
56	4000	76	4380	83	4149	64	16.89	16.82	17.73
57	3924	82	4297	85	4085	63	16.21	16.14	17.00
58	3842	93	4212	78	4022	93	15.55	15.45	16.25
59	3749	106	4134	116	3929	61	14.92	14.73	15.63
60	3643	122	4018	135	3868	59	14.34	14.14	14.87
61	3521	126	3883	86	3809	61	13.82	13.62	14.09
62	3395	127	3797	99	3748	119	13.31	12.91	13.31
63	3268	125	3698	177	3629	114	12.81	12.25	12.73
64	3143	125	3521	98	3515	112	12.30	11.84	12.13
65	3018	124	3423	132	3403	191	11.79	11.16	11.52
66	2894	123	3291	177	3212	132	11.27	10.59	11.17
67	2771	123	3114	156	3080	101	10.75	10.16	10.63
68	2648	123	2958	146	2979	185	10.23	9.67	9.97
69	2525	124	2812	194	2794	109	9.70	9.15	9.61
70	2401	124	2618	159	2685	316	9.18	8.79	8.98
71	2277	134	2459	147	2369	86	8.65	8.33	9.13
72	2143	146	2312	234	2283	124	8.16	7.83	8.46
73	1997	156	2078	151	2159	100	7.72	7.65	7.92
74	1841	166	1927	179	2059	168	7.33	7.21	7.29
75	1675	160	1748	181	1891	245	7.01	6.90	6.90
76	1515	156	1567	120	1646	100	6.69	6.63	6.85
77	1359	146	1447	106	1546	80	6.40	6.15	6.26
78	1213	132	1341	113	1466	142	6.12	5.59	5.58
79	1081	128	1228	120	1324	194	5.80	5.06	5.12
80	953	116	1108	204	1130	221	5.51	4.55	4.91
81	837	112	904	190	909	149	5.21	4.47	4.98
82	725	102	714	61	762	94	4.93	4.53	4.84
83	623	94	653	113	668	62	4.65	3.90	4.43
84	529	84	540	100	606	102	4.39	3.61	3.84
85	445	78	440	95	504	98	4.12	3.32	3.52
86	367	71	345	79	406	84	3.90	3.10	3.25
87	296	64	266	61	322	73	3.71	2.88	2.96
88	232	51	205	55	249	60	3.59	2.58	2.69
89	181	39	150	40	189	55	3.47	2.35	2.38

Continued

Age	Carlisle Table.		Ministers' Widows' Fund.				Expectation of Life		
			Males		Females		Carlisle	Ministers' Fund	
	Living	Dying	Living	Dying	Living	Dying		Males.	Females.
90	142	37	110	33	134	42	3.28	2.02	2.15
91	105	30	77	28	92	33	3.26	1.67	1.90
92	75	21	49	22	59	25	3.37	1.34	1.69
93	54	14	27	17	34	14	3.48	1.02	1.56
94	40	10	10	7	20	11	3.53	.90	1.30
95	30	7	3	2	9	5	3.53	.83	1.28
96	23	5	1	1	4	2	3.46	.50	1.25
97	18	4	...	...	2	1	3.28	...	1.00
98	14	3	...	...	1	1	3.07	...	.50

In recording the statistics, each life was exposed for the years and fraction of a year during which he was a member. The resulting rates of mortality were not graduated, but were used to prepare a table commencing at age 21 showing how a number of persons would die off under rates of mortality similar to that of the Ministers' Widows' Fund. Commenting on the results Thomson wrote:

"In the earlier ages from 30 to 44, the expectation of life among males, it will be perceived, is considerably in favour of the Ministers' Widows' Fund, but this is probably owing to the select nature of the lives which enter the church, contrasted with an observation on a general population; but from 44 to 75, the two tables approximate so closely, as to support each other entirely—the value of life, however, appearing to be on the whole in favour of the Carlisle, but to such a small extent as to be scarcely appreciable in the average gross result. If the columns of the expectation of life be summed up for the period between 44 and 75, both inclusive, the following result is obtained—

Sum of expectation of life according to Carlisle Tables   488.80
    do.   do.   according to Ministers' Widows' Fund (Males) 477.87

Or upon the whole about one-third of a years' purchase in favour of the Carlisle Table upon each year's value.

After 75, the value of life is greater by the Carlisle Table; but this portion of the Carlisle Table is generally supposed to shew too great an expectation of life, and I have no doubt the results deduced from the Ministers' Widows' Fund are nearer the truth.

It will also be perceived that I have made a separate observation on the value of Female life in the Scheme, and the expectation shewn by the calculation is given in a separate column; the result being that Female life is at least of 5 per cent more value than Male life. Thus, comparing the results between 44 and 75, we find—

Sum of expectation of life according to Ministers' Widows' Fund (Females)		508.28
do. do.	(Males)	477.87
	Difference	30.41

Or above 6 per cent in favour of females.

Having thus tested the accuracy of the Carlisle Tables as regards the probable value of Male life, as compared with the Ministers' Widows' Fund, and having ascertained the extent of which Female life is better than Male life in the Scheme, I at once deemed it right to adopt the Carlisle Tables as the basis of my calculations, giving effect to the difference in value of Female life."

The change in the method of valuation had rendered inappropriate the particular instructions laid down in the Act for accumulation of Funds and determination of surplus. The Act, however, was quite definite on the disposal of surplus—only two-thirds of the free revenue on the surplus being available to increase annuities. Assuming a return of 4% this meant that not more than £842 could be added to annuities on this occasion and this was sufficient to increase annuities in payment by only £2. As Thomson reported: "It is not a large sum, and it will afford but a small increase to the annuitants, but I am much impressed by the view that in a Fund like this, in which Justice is expected to hold the scales, not sacrificing the present to the future, or the future for the present, but dealing even-handed justice to all, small divisions should not be despised."

The next valuation was due, at the earliest, in 1875 and in that year the trustees asked James Meikle to prepare a report. Meikle's report, in print, extends to 60 pages of A4 and contains a wealth of interesting statistics of which but a few can be mentioned here. He compared the mortality of widows and contributors for the period with what would have been expected from a variety of tables with the following results:

Table	Actual deaths as %age of expected
	Contributors
Halley's	71
English Life No. 3	97
Carlisle	107
Assured Lives	102
Healthy Districts of England	102
Church of England Clergy	102
	Widows
Carlisle	86
Governments Annuitants (Female)	113

Meikle showed the selection which was being exercised against the Fund, married members selecting a higher rate of annuity than unmarried and the older the member the higher the annuity chosen. The mortality among members selecting the lowest annuity was substantially lighter than the average. He also investigated the effect of new entrants on the finances of the Fund. After crediting new entrants with a share of the expected revenue from vacant stipends, he found that new entrants were more than self-supporting up to age 31 at entry, but above that age their entry increased the liabilities of the Fund. Over the period the total value of contributions from new entrants, including allowance for vacant stipends, exceeded the value of benefits by 13%. If vacant stipends were excluded, there would have been a deficiency of 10%.

Meikle expressed some doubts as to the interpretation of

the 1814 Act with regard to the disposal of surplus. He considered it would be equivalent but more appropriate to make an additional reserve of $7\frac{1}{2}$% of the net liability and to use the balance of surplus to increase annuities by such an amount as it would support. In the event he was able to recommend an increase of £2.

By a decision of the court of Session in 1849 it was found that a minister of a Parliamentary church which had been erected into a parish quod sacra (that is, where the Kirk Session was only responsible for spiritual supervision and not financial matters), and who had been inducted into it before it was erected, was not entitled to become a contributor. It was assumed that this decision would bar all such ministers, but a further judgement with reference to St Margaret's, Edinburgh ruled that all ministers were eligible. Accordingly the investigation which might have been made in 1889 was postponed as the trustees were applying for an Act to regularise the position. This was granted in 1890 and as the ministers concerned were given a year to decide whether or not to join, the investigation was not made until 1891. During the previous 38 years, 232 quoad sacra parishes had been erected and in 1891 there were 118 ministers and 15 surviving widows eligible to join the Fund. In fact 38 ministers opted to join and Meikle calculated the additional liability for these and the 15 widows to be £12,000. As a result of this and a fall in the rate of interest he was unable to recommend any increase in annuities.

In 1904 Archibald Hewat, another past president of the Faculty of Actuaries, was asked to undertake an investigation. Hewat had already investigated the experience of the Fund for ministers of the Free Church of Scotland for the period 1845 to 1900 and he used the tables he had prepared from that experience for comparison. As the differences found were not great, he was able to use the Free Church experience in his valuation. For the first time, an item "Provision for new entrants" appeared in the valuation balance sheet. It was the sum which he estimated was necessary to meet the liabilities which new entrants in succeeding years would bring upon the Fund beyond that which could be met from entry monies, annual rates, marriage-taxes and their share of vacant stipends. Contributions from new entrants were then, on average, meeting only 83% of the cost of their benefits. This was perhaps the time when contributions should have been revised, but the opportunity was missed to the detriment of the future level of benefits. Hewat thought that a more accurate interpretation of the 1814 Act required one-third of the surplus to be reserved and from the balance recommended an increase of £3 in all annuities.

The next investigation was due in 1918 and was carried out by Alexander Fraser. Interest rates had risen during the period, particularly in the latter years of the First World War, and he was able to increase the rate of interest assumed in the valuation from 3% to 4%. The result was a considerable release of reserves and he was able to recommend an increase in annuities of £10 per annum. In the event the trustees decided not to hold a specific reserve for future expenses and increased annuities by £12. In his report he recorded the unusual case of a widow who died in 1910 in her 107th year having survived her husband by 74 years. Fraser recommended that future investigations be made at intervals of 7 years and was again asked to report in 1925. In the meantime a new Act had been obtained in 1923 which made a number of minor changes which are detailed elsewhere. Perhaps the most significant change was in the distribution of surplus which reverted to the original practice of increasing annuities in proportion to annual rates. For the first time it was possible to examine the mortality experience of the wives of contributors, and this was found to be much lighter than the Free Church experience and more in line with the Scottish Bankers experience. Additions were recommended to the four classes of £2, £3, £4 and £5 respectively. In 1928, after more than twenty years of discussion, agreement was in sight for a union of the United Free Church and the Church of Scotland. The ministers of the former were members of the Free Churches (Scotland) Widows' and Orphans' Fund and indeed formed the majority of its membership. Accordingly the trustees of both Schemes asked their actuaries, Alexander Fraser and Andrew Rutherford Davidson, to report on the feasibility of amalgamating the two funds. They reported that such an arrangement could be carried out on the following lines:

(a) The investments and other assets of the two funds should be merged for all purposes.
(b) The contributors to each Fund before the merger should continue to pay the same rates and enjoy benefits determined in the same manner as hitherto. In order to determine the relative levels of benefit a valuation of each Fund should be made on the same basis.
(c) Future entrants into the common Fund should pay contributions and receive benefits, if possible, identical with or nearly so to those of one or other of the existing Funds. The Scheme of the Free Church, being more modern and simpler, was suggested.

Fraser and Davidson were asked to proceed with the valuations and produce a more detailed scheme. The basis for valuation presented little problem as the experienced rates of mortality, marriage and interest were not dissimilar. The previous valuation of the Church of Scotland Fund had been made at 4% compared with $3\frac{3}{4}$% in the case of the Free Church Fund, but the additional reserve of one-third of surplus in the former was not very different from what would have been required to increase reserves to the lower interest basis. A common rate of 4% was used with additional contingency reserves of the same order percentage-wise as the surplus held back in the previous Church of Scotland valuation.

The main difference between the Funds lay in the treatment of vacant stipends, since the Free Church Fund was only entitled to an annual rate during a vacancy while the Church of Scotland Fund could receive the whole stipend. It was suggested that the Free Church practice be adopted in future and that the Church of Scotland Fund be compensated by a series of fixed payments. On the basis of an average of £3,000 vacant stipends the actuaries suggested 40 annual paymens of £3,789 and eventually the Church agreed to a figure of £3,500. The value of these payments was included in the valuation as an asset of the Church of Scotland Fund.

As regards new entrants, both Funds were in the same

position, the value of benefits was greater than the value of contributions and reserves were required for future entrants. As a result of the valuations, increases were recommended to the annuities in both Funds. The combined valuation balance sheet was then shown as being capable of supporting the new rates of annuity and new entrants who would have been entitled to enter either of the Funds had there been no amalgamation. The new entrants were to enjoy the same benefits as provided by the old Free Church Fund and pay the same annual rate of £7. Future surplus was first to be divided between pre-union Church of Scotland members and the rest in proportion to the gross value of benefits. The pre-union portion was then to be divided in proportion to annual rates and the remainder in proportion to annuities.

Fraser and Davidson then turned their attention to the question of the admission of Church of Scotland missionaries, chaplains and clergymen in the Synod in England and in the Church overseas. As regards the entry of the successors of these classes, it was estimated that an additional liability of £5,000 would arise, but that this was not significant in relation to the common Fund of £2,100,000. As regards the present ministers in these classes, however, it was recommended that they be admitted at special rates of contribution so that they introduce no liability to the common Fund. The recommendations were approved, and the amalgamation, with effect from 2nd October 1929, was constituted by Provisional Order in 1930.

The changes in annuities during the period were as follows:

Class	Increase in Annuity						Total Annuity
	1863	1877	1906	1920	1927	1929	
	£	£	£	£	£	£ s.d.	£ s. d.
I	2	2	3	12	2	1.10.0	44.10.0
II	2	2	3	12	3	2. 5.0	54. 5.0
III	2	2	3	12	4	3. 0.0	64. 0.0
IV	2	2	3	12	5	3.15.0	73.15.0
Free Church						2. 0. 0	66. 0.0
New Entrants							66. 0.0

The total annuities payable in 1929 may be compared with the minimum stipend at the time, which was £300 plus a manse.

SINCE 1930

The Churches and Universities (Scotland)
Widows' and Orphans' Fund

CHAPTER 8

Changes since 1930

[For Acts of Parliament, see Appendix 1, pp 135-146.]

The Act of Parliament 20 & 21 Geo. V Cap XXXIV (1930) confirmed the Provisional Order under the Private Legislation Procedure (Scotland) Act 1899 on 1st August 1930. The Church of Scotland Ministers' and Scottish Universities' Widows' Fund and the Free Churches' (Scotland) Widows' and Orphans' Fund were amalgamated. There were two sections, the General Fund and the old Church of Scotland Fund which continued with its old provisions for widows and orphans of those who had made choices of rate before the Act. The £7 rate of the Free Church Scheme continued in the General Fund for all new entrants, ministers, missionaries and professors. Entry money of £10 if not more than 35, and £15 for others, was payable. Marriage-Tax was £10 plus £1 for each year by which age exceeded the age of the wife.

A new Act was passed in 1954 and this, amended in 1967 and 1981, is still in force. It is very detailed. It continued the 1930 Act as to the appointment of trustees (ministers and elders), twelve appointed by the Church of Scotland General Assembly, four by the Free Church General Assembly and four professors appointed by the Court of the University of Edinburgh. The main changes were that chaplains to the forces were made eligible to join the Fund, legally adopted children were entitled to benefit and wider powers of investment were granted to the trustees.

There was a gradual movement away from investment in land securities at commissioners' rates and feu duties.

In 1967 an amending Act was passed, providing that no

more professors should be admitted to the Fund, other than church professors.

Since proper investment of capital is so important, it was decided in 1970 to employ Messrs. Martin Currie, after regular meetings with the trustees, to manage the day to day investment of the capital of the Fund. The bulk of the capital was now in stocks and shares. By 1980 heritable loans had been phased out.

In 1979 the trustees decided, out of benevolent funds, to make payment of a Christmas bonus to all widows in their care.

In 1977 it was decided that triennial actuarial investigations should replace quinquennial, so that widows might more quickly benefit from a rising asset.

In 1981 Parliament confirmed another Provisional Order amending the Act of 1954. This resulted from the Finance Act of 1970 and the admission of women to the ministry of the Church of Scotland. Chaplains to the Forces were no longer eligible for membership and women had the option of joining. Wider powers of investment were granted to the trustees. No more payments were to be made by those who had left the service of the Churches.

In 1984, after conference with a Committee of the Church of Scotland, ways were examined to reduce the expenses of the Fund. With the invaluable help of Mr Eric Hubbard steps were taken to this end. In 1988 all the feu duties were sold to the Church of Scotland. The Trust's Offices at 137a George Street were sold for £510,000 and room was found at 121 George Street. Computerisation meant that the Clerk and Treasurer has nobly managed to operate on his own and considerable savings have been made.

Arrangements have recently been made for entry money on a sliding scale to be added to the annual rates and spread through the whole period of payment and, where possible, by deduction from stipend by the Churches.

There are still in care of the Fund, some widows whose husbands joined before 1930, who receive one of four payments dependent on choice of one of four rates in the old Church of Scotland Scheme.

CHAPTER 9

Actuarial Aspects of the Fund in Recent Years

George C Philip FFA

The experience of the Fund since the Union in 1929 may best be considered in two periods. In the first period from 1929 to 1954 the main feature was the low rate of return obtainable on investments. In 1929 70% of the assets was invested in loans on heritable property, 27% in Government Stocks and 3% in feu duties. By 1954, the percentage invested in property loans had been reduced to 56%, while that in feu duties had increased to 7%, and in Government Stocks and other fixed interest securities to 35%. The balance of 2% was invested in the ordinary stock of Scottish banks. Over the whole of this period the average return on assets was under 4%, and consequently while A E King in his valuation in 1935 was able to assume a rate of interest of $3\frac{3}{4}\%$, R L Gwilt in 1944 and 1949 felt obliged to reduce the rate to $3\frac{1}{4}\%$. The result was a substantial increase in the reserve required for all future entrants to cover the deficiency in their contributions assuming that the annual rate remained fixed. In 1944, for example, the reserve required for new entrants was £610,000, equivalent to 25% of total assets. It was pointed out in successive actuarial reports that not only did each new entrant bring a liability on to the Fund, but that this liability increased every time the annuity was increased. This situation continued until the granting of the 1954 Order which permitted annual rates to be increased, but only for new entrants. Gwilt in 1954 recommended an increase in the annual rate for new entrants from £7 to £10.50, but by then the equivalent of

123

the original £7 in purchasing power was £17.50 and the equivalent of the £66 annuity would have been £165 but it was only £95.

The period from 1954 was one of increasing interest rates, unfortunately accompanied by periods of high inflation. Until 1979 the annuity from the Fund was the only provision made by the Churches for widows and it was, therefore, vital that it be kept at as high a level as possible. The need to maximise secure income acted as a constraint on the investment policy of the trustees since it limited the extent to which they could accept the lower initial yield on equities, although the intrinsic value of such investments was already recognised. In 1970 the investments of the Fund still consisted largely of British Government securities, Loan stocks, Feu-duties and Bonds on property, only 12.6% being in ordinary stocks and shares. By 1989, however, Feu-duties and Bonds on heritable property had been eliminated from the portfolio and 65% of the total invested was in ordinary shares.

In 1959 Gwilt, and in 1964 A F Ross, found that contributions by new entrants were only covering two-thirds of the cost of their benefits and modest increases in the annual rate were recommended. The annual rate was still, however, the same for all ages at entry. The pattern of recruitment for the ministry was changing and entrants were increasingly coming in at older ages with consequent additional liability to the Fund. To compensate for this the Amending Order of 1967 gave power to the Trustees to increase entry monies and marriage-taxes. This was recommended by Ross after the 1969 investigation but it was not found practical to raise entry monies to a level which would make older entrants self-supporting without requiring lump sums which were beyond the means of the ministers who were obliged to join the Scheme. Nevertheless, with increases in annual rates, marriage-taxes and entry monies, and with the higher rates of interest which could now be assumed in valuations, the reserve for new entrants was greatly reduced. The need for it finally disappeared with the Amending Order of 1980 which made the changes necessary for the Fund to be approved under the Finance Act 1970 and enjoy exemption from all taxes. The principal changes were the requirement for contributions from future entrants to cease at age 65 and the immediate cessation of contributions from members who were no longer in the service of the Churches or Universities. The first of these effectively abolished the principle of a uniform rate for all, irrespective of age, and opened the way for an annual contribution, including entry money, based on age and sufficient to support the basic annuity at entry. The members who were required to cease contributions were given retained benefits according to their contribution record and expressed as a percentage of the normal annuity, and this practice has been continued for subsequent leavers.

However, as the reserve for new entrants was reduced, it was, unfortunately, necessary to replace it with an increasing reserve for future expenses. Due to inflation, administration expenses, which in 1970 represented 36% of the contribution income, had risen to 96% of such income by 1988. Since then, however, the Fund's own premises have been sold at a handsome profit and the administration moved into an office within the Church of Scotland offices and a considerable reduction in expenses has been achieved. In 1991, administration expenses had fallen to 48% of contribution income.

The following extracts from the Actuarial Report on the Fund as at 15 May 1992, show the progress that has been made in recent years:

STATISTICS OF MEMBERSHIP

	1974	1977	1980	1983	1986	1989	1992
Contributors	3,082	2,980	2,931	2,903	2,871	2,888	2,829
Widows	968	951	914	909	929	922	901

The 1992 figure for contributions includes 514 members with retained benefits after ceasing to contribute.

ASSETS OF THE FUND

As at 15th May 1992 the assets of the Fund were as Follows:-

Loan Stocks and Debentures	£1,702,299
Convertible Loan Stocks	599,838
Equities	7,802,508
Stock Exchange Securities at market value	£10,034,645
Cash and Deposits	617,417
Debtors less Creditors	40,541
	£10,692,603

RESULTS OF VALUATION

The results of the valuation as at 15th May 1992 are as follows:-
Value of:

Assets		£10,692,000
Future annual rates		542,000
Future marriage rates and contributions for vacant charges		30,000
		11,264,000

Less value of:

Benefits to current pensioners	£3,839,000	
Benefits to future pensioners	4,515,000	
Provision for expenses	321,000	8,675,000
Valuation surplus		£2,589,000

RECOMMENDATIONS

Basic Annuities

I recommend that the above surplus be used to increase the basic annuities with effect from May 1993 as follows:-

	Current Basic Annuity 1992 £	Temporary Addition 1992 £	Proposed Basic Annuity 1993 £
General Fund	545.00	138.40	710.00
Pre-Union Class I	301.49	76.63	390.10
" " II	439.86	111.66	572.91
" " III	577.89	146.79	755.10
" " IV	715.98	181.74	937.50

CHAPTER 10

Churches and Universities (Scotland) Widows' and Orphans' Fund Trustees

F	=	Member Finance Committee
Res.	=	Resigned
U	=	Universities
Free	=	Free Church of Scotland

First Trustees 1930

Very Rev. John	J D MacCallum DD	Died before first meeting
Rev.	James T Cox DD	Died 1948
Rev.	Arthur S Middleton BD	F Res. 1948 Died 1949
	William Galbraith WS	*Chairman* 1930–33 F Res. 1937
Rev.	George Macaulay DD	Died 1938
Rev.	James Weatherhead DD	Died 1944
Rev.	John S Ewen BD BSc	F Died 1941
	Archibald B Campbell WS	F Died 1940
	Steuart B Hog of Newliston	Res. 1935
	John Parker Watson WS	F 1930–35 Res. 1935
	Hamilton Maxwell WS	Died 1932
	John T Sherriff Watson CA	F Died 1936
	William Rounsfell Brown (Free)	F Res. 1947
Rev. Prof.	Donald MacLean DD (Free)	Died 1943
Rev.	Alexander Stewart DD (Free)	Died 1937
	Donald MacCallum Smith WS (Free)	F Died 1950
Prof.	James Mackintosh KC BA LLD (U)	Res. 1937
Prof.	Sir Ernest Maclagan Wedderburn LLB DSc Kt.1962, WS DKS (U)	*Chairman* 1937–51 Res. F 1951
Prof.	Robert Candlish Henderson KC LLB (U)	F Res. 1947
Prof.	John Girvan LLB (U)	Died 1946
Very Rev.	Joseph Mitchell DD (in lieu Dr MacCallum)	Died 1931

Year	Title	Name	Notes
1931	Very Rev.	J Montgomery Campbell DD	Died 1937
1932		Arthur W Russell WS	F 1932 Res. 1958
1935	Rev.	J Ford McLeod BD	F 1936 Died 1964
1935	Prof.	William Wilson	Died 1944
1936	Prof.	Alexander MacKelvie CA	F 1936 Died 1956
1937	Rev.	H H Monteath LLB WS (U)	F 1940 Res. 1955
		Frank H Martin BD	Died 1941
		John Shaw MA (Free)	Died 1950
		Norman MacLeod CMG DSO DL CA	Res. 1957
1938	Rev.	J R Aitken DD	Died 1943
1940		William D Macdougall MA LLB	Res. 1943
1941		Albert A Diack	Res. 1957 Died 1958
	Rev.	R E McIntyre BD DD	Died 1961
	Rev.	Oliver Russell DD	Died 1952
1943	Rev.	David McKenzie MA (Free)	Res. 1973
	Prof.	A Wallace Cowan JP FRSA	Res. 1955
1944	Rev.	John Sinclair BD DD	Died 1970
	Prof.	Matthew G Fisher KC MA LLB QC CBE	F *Chairman* 1951–65 Died 1965
1946	Prof.	John Boyd LLB (U)	Res. 1957
1947		John W Baxter BCom (Free)	Died 1961
	Prof.	George A Montgomery KC LLB (U)	F 1947–57 & 58 Res. 1968
1946	Rev.	Thomas Caldwell DD PhD	Res. 1958
	Rev.	R C M Mathers MA	Res. 1970

Year	Title	Name	Notes
1950	Rev.	William McLeod MA (Free)	Res. 1953
1951		D MacArthur, Solicitor (Free)	Died 1964
1952	Rev.	Simon Fraser WS	Res. 1960
1953	Rev. Prof.	A Ian Dunlop TD, MA BD	F 1956–*Chairman* 1965-
		W J Cameron MA, BD (Free)	F 1967 Res. 1988 Died 1990
1955		F H N Walker CA	F, Convener F 1965–74 Res. 1979 Died 1986
1956	Prof.	A A Matheson MA LLB (U)	Res. 1966
1957		John M Ross FFA FRSE	F Res. 1973
	Prof.	E M Wright BA MA DPhil (U)	Res. 1963
1958	Prof.	J M Halliday MA LLB (U)	F 1958 Res. 1971
	Rev.	Harold C M Eggo TD MA	F 1973 Res. 1978 Died 1991
1960		J Y Simpson MA BCom	F 1965 Died 1967
	Rev.	Leonard E Dickson CBE MC LLB TD DL	Res. 1991
		J S Ritchie WS	F Res. 1988
1961		James Stewart(Free)	Res. 1976
		James Bremner Dow MA FFA	F Convener F 1974–82 Res. 1983 Died 1987
1963		E M Phemister DSc FRS (U)	Res. 1972
1964	Prof.	G B C Sangster DSC BD	F 1978 Res. 1980
	Rev.	D A Cameron BL (Free)	F 1967 Res. 1986
1965		George W Burnet LLB WS	F 1965

Year	Title	Name	Status
1966	Rev. Principal	Matthew Black MA DD DLitt FBA (U)	Res. 1978
1967	Rev.	Alwyn J C Macfarlane MA	Res. 1979
1969	Prof.	G L F Henry BL WS (U)	F Res. 1989
1970	Rev.	J Forbes Macdonald CA BD	Died 1971
	Rev.	A A McArthur MA BD PhD	Died 1986
1971	Prof.	Allan D Galloway BD STM PhD (U)	Res. 1979
	Rev.	David H Whiteford CBE BD PhD	F 1987
	Prof.	R C Cross	Res. 1976
1972	Rev. Prof.	John McIntyre DD DLitt	Res. 1977
1973	Rev. Prof.	N M Collins BA BD DD (Free)	F Res. 1989 Died 1989
1974	Prof.	Maxwell Gaskin DFC MA (U)	Res. 1985
1976		Iain D Gill CA ATII (Free)	F
1977	Prof.	G W Anderson DD DTheol FBA (U)	Res. 1981
1978	Rev.	George L Lugton MA BD	F Res. 1988
1979	Very. Rev. Prof.	James A Whyte MA LLB (U)	Res. 1990
	Rev.	Colin G F Brockie BSc BD	
1980		Patrick J Burnet CA	F Convener F 1982–
	Prof.	Ernest Best MA BD PhD	Res. 1983
	Rev.	D Hugh Davidson MA	
1981	Rev. Prof.	Duncan B Forrester MA BD DPhil (U)	F Res. 1987
1983	Prof.	D C Gilles BSc PhD FRSE FIMA (U)	F
	Lt. Col.	Thomas D S Bell TD BL SSC DL	Res. 1990
1985	Rev. Prof.	James B Torrance MA BD (U)	
1986		Alastair Macdonald OBE (Free)	

1986	Rev.	Andrew R C McLellan MA BD STM	F
1987	Rev.	Principal C Graham MA BD (Free)	F
	Prof.	Archibald A M Duncan MA SBA FRHistS FRSE	Res. 1990
1988	Prof.	Ewan Brown MA LLB CA	F
	Rev.	James L. Weatherhead MA LLB	F
1989		Ewan K Cameron WS	F
1989	Rev. Prof.	William Johnstone MA BD (U)	F
1989	Rev. Prof.	George M Newlands MA BD PhD (U)	
1990	Rev. Prof.	John L MacKay MA MLitt BD (Free)	F
1990	Rev. Principal	D W D Shaw BA BD LLB WS DD (U)	
1991		Graham D M Reid BL	
1992	Prof.	Richard Henry Roberts BA MA PhD	

Officers of the Fund since 1930

Treasurers

C E W McPherson (C of S 1897) CA (Joint) N. St David St. 1930, Died 1931
W A A Balfour CA (Free 1894) (Joint) Castle St. 1930, Died 1932
Thomas S Martin CA 1933, Died 1940
A Scott Lawrie (Joint) 1940, Died 1941
F P Milligan WS (Joint) 1940–1957
John McPherson (Joint) 1941–1957
Henry A Younger 1957–1974, Died 1980
Ronald H Bradly FAAI 1974–1983, Died 1983
Eric Hubbard IPFA FCCA 1984–

Law Agents

F P Milligan WS (Clerk and Law Agent) (Joint Clerk 1930–39) 1930–60, Died 1960
Alex P Melville WS Joint Clerk 1930–39, Died 1939
L R S Mackenzie WS 1960–1985
A I Arnot WS 1985–

Actuaries

A E King FFA FIA Investigation 1935
R L Gwilt CBE FFA FIA FRSE Investigations 1940, 1944, 1949, 1954, 1959
A F Ross FFA Investigations 1964, 1969
G C Philip FFA Investigations 1974, 1977, 1980, 1983, 1986, 1989, 1991

Auditors

George Fraser CA (Joint) 1930–1936, Died 1936
Edward Boyd CA (Joint 1930–1948 A K McKelvie CA 1949–1986

David H Sclater CA 1967
Robert D Darling CA 1968–1986
D S Donnan BA CA 1987–1988
Brian Marshall BCom CA 1989–

Principal Office Staff

Miss Agnes S Anderson, Retired 1959 (after 50 years)
Miss A K Scott 1958–1976
Mrs Chapman 1975–1982
Mrs Pilley 1982–1988

APPENDIX 1

The Acts of Parliament

A Summary of Provisions

J S Ritchie WS

['Principal Acts are indicated by an asterisk.]

*The ACT 17 GEO. II. (1744) entitled *"An Act for raising and establishing a Fund for a Provision for the Widows and Children of the Ministers of the Church of Scotland and of the Heads, Principals and Masters of the Universities of Saint Andrews, Glasgow and Edinburgh"*—narrated that the widows and children of the ministers of the Church and of the heads, principals and masters in the Universities of Scotland had often been left in indigent circumstances without any provision for their subsistence or education.

The Act provided that such ministers, heads, principals and masters were to pay, out of their stipends or salaries, at their option, rates of either £2:12:6, £3:18:9, £5:5/- or £6:11:3, with an additional payment equal to the annual rate on the first and each succeeding marriage, which sums were to be applied for payment of liferent annuities to widows of, depending on the rate chosen, £10, £15, £20 or £25 and for provision for children, where there was no widow, of a capital sum equal to ten times the appropriate widow's annuity (under deduction of any sum paid to the widow where she survived her husband but died within ten years of him). The Act further provided that the surplus of the rates, after payment of widows' annuities and childrens' provisions, was to be lent out to the extent of £30 to each minister and university professor, repayable on his ceasing to hold his charge or office and any further surpluses were to be lent out on proper security until the capital should be made up to £35,000.

135

The foregoing Act was explained and amended by the ACT
22 GEO. II (1749) which brought the heads, principals and
masters of the University of Aberdeen into the Fund. The
authorised capital was raised to £50,000 over and above the
sums of £30 lent to ministers and professors.

*The ACT 19 GEO. III CAP. 20 (1779) repealed the two previous
Acts and, with variation and considerable, mainly administrative, amplification re-enacted them. The Act narrated
that it had been found from experience that the granting of a
loan of £30 each to the ministers and professors had, in many
instances, proved hurtful to their families and to the Fund,
and further that the interest of a larger stock or capital
would be necessary for the support of the Fund. It accordingly provided that it would not thenceforward be competent
for ministers or professors to demand, nor for the trustees
to grant, loans of £30 and it raised the authorised capital to
£100,000, this sum to be made up by the accumulation of
annual surpluses. The Act made membership of the Fund
compulsory for life notwithstanding loss of status, resigna-
tion of appointment, deprivation or any other eventuality.
Those joining the Fund, aged forty and over, were to pay
$2\frac{1}{2}$ rates on marriage. A half-year's rate was to be payable
on the death of every minister or professor, payable from
the Ann (the right of the widow or next-of-kin of a deceased
minister to a half-year's stipend) where this was competent
and otherwise by the deceased's heir. When a benefice or
University office was vacant, a sum of £3.2.6 per half year
was to be payable.

The ACT 54 GEO. III CAP. 169 (1814) amended the Act of 1779.
It narrated that the capital had been duly made up to
£100,000 and that the contributors, on being called upon to
give an opinion as to future disposal of surplus revenue had
determined that it should be applied solely to the benefit of
the widows of the contributors. The narrative continued:

"And whereas from the encreased Expence of Living
and Decrease in the Value of Money, the Annuities and
Provisions fixed by the said recited Act are found to be
now totally inadequate to the support of the Widows and
Children of Ministers and Professors; and it has become

expedient, for the purpose of remedying this great and encreasing Evil, and to prevent the Recurrence of a similar Urgency, to make certain Alterations on the said recited Act and on the annual Rates thereby made payable . . .''

Therefore the various annual rates were increased by 20 per cent to £3:3/-, £4:14:6, £6:6/- and £7:17:6, marriage-taxes being similarly increased. It was further narrated that a great majority of the contributors had entered into a subscription to raise an additional sum for the purposes of the Act and that every new contributor on admission should pay £10 as being nearly the average of the original subscriptions. It was enacted that when a parish became vacant after 1813, the stipend should thereafter be paid to the Fund.

Steps were taken by the Act to provide beneficiaries of the Fund with a steady and increasing income and thus to enable them to combat the rising cost of living. Since surpluses had arisen in each year they had been divided and added to the annuities, but experience had shown that these surpluses varied considerably from year to year "whereby the Widows are left in uncertainty as to the Extent of the Income which they are to receive in any one Year." Accordingly the trustees were directed to ascertain the average of the surplus since it began to be divided, which average was to be fixed as the sum to be divided amongst the widows then on the Fund and the proportion of such surplus was to be the sum to be paid thereafter in each year to each widow on the Fund along with the original annuity.

The Act then provided that any further surpluses, together with the subscription previously mentioned, donations and the increased rates and further sums payable under the Act were, with any annual excess on the average surplus, to form a capital fund to be invested in loans on good security, in Government Funds or in land, the income to be accumulated for six years; and thereafter along with the twenty per cent increase in rates to be distributed annually to the widows and orphans under the age of 18 in the proportion to the rates chosen by their husbands or fathers. Again there was provision for fixing the amount to be paid by averaging the income of the preceding six years.

The Act went on to provide for a second accumulation for six years of the money raised by the subscription of contributors, the sums appointed to be paid by future incumbents corresponding to the average of the original subscriptions (£10), produce of vacant stipends and other donations and sums becoming due; at the end of the accumulation period such yearly sum as the trustees might think expedient, not exceeding two-thirds of the revenue, was again to be added to the annuities, but in this case equally and without regard to the class of contributions paid by the husbands or fathers.

Following this second addition the unappropriated part of the capital fund was to be accumulated for a further period of not less than 14 years when a further sum was to be divided in the same manner as for the second addition. This accumulation procedure was to be repeated in all time thereafter, the accumulation period in each case being not less than 14 years; and similar additional sums, in the trustees' discretion, were to be applied for the benefit of the widows and orphans "care being always had not to circumscribe too much the Operation of the Capital Fund or Stock, it being always the true Meaning and Intent of this Act that there shall always belong to such Capital Fund or Stock such a Sum or Revenue as may admit from Time to Time of the Advance to the Annuities of the Widows and Orphan Families of Contributors in some Degree corresponding to what may be the encreased Expence of Living and to the consequent Exigencies of their Situation"—an early attempt to combat the continuing problem of inflation.

The trustees were required to subjoin to their annual report to the General Assembly of the Church of Scotland a General Statement of the Fund created under this Act.

Minor amendments to the Acts of 1779 and 1814 were made by the ACT 53 & 54 VICT. CAP. 124 (1890). This Act (the first to be given the facility of a short title—"*The Church of Scotland Ministers' Widows' Fund Act 1890*"—was passed to regularise the position following upon apparently conflicting interpretations of the situation arising on the erection of a charge into a parish quoad sacra. In 1849 the Court of Session, in an action at the instance of the Collector against the minister of the church and parish of Kinlochspelvie which had been erected into a parish quoad sacra found

> ". . . that ministers ordained and admitted to the charge of any church and district after the same shall have been erected into a church and parish quoad sacra . . . are bound and entitled to become contributors to the ministers' widows' fund but . . . that parties holding the charge of any church and district so erected, but who have been appointed to the same before the date of such erection, are not bound or entitled to become contributors to the fund."

In 1887, however, the Court of Session in a special case presented on behalf of the Collector and the minister of the quoad sacra parish of St Margaret's, Edinburgh found that the minister who had officiated at the church of St Margaret's before it had been erected into a parish quoad sacra, and acted as minister after the date of erection, was bound and entitled to be a contributor to the Fund. To remedy the confusion, the Act provided that where a person had acted as officiating minister of a chapel or place of worship within a district prior to its being erected as a parish quoad sacra or quoad omnia and, before the passing of the Act, had been recognised as the first minister of the created parish, such person should be entitled to claim to be a contributor to the Fund as from the date of erection of the parish. In this case he would be bound to pay the annual rates and other payments with interest from the dates when these would have become due and that, where a minister who would, had he survived, have been entitled under the Act to claim to be a contributor, had died, his widow or children were to be entitled to the annuity appropriate to a rate of £4:14:6—but under deduction of the sums with interest which the husband or father would have paid had he been a contributor, but excluding arrears relating to a period more than five years prior to the passing of the Act.

The Church of Scotland Ministers' and Scottish University Professors' Widows' Fund Order Confirmation Act, 1923 (ACT 13 & 14 GEO. V.—SESSION 1923) repealed the Acts of 1779 to

1890 and consolidated and amended the statutory provisions relating to the Fund. Rates were to be payable throughout life. Marriage-tax was to equal the annual rate; but for contributors over age 40 on admission, if married, or widowers with children, was to be two and a half times the annual rate. The funds were to be applied in payment of (a) annuities to widows on the Fund; (b) annuities to widows of contributors dying thereafter; and (c) provisions to children. Children were to be entitled to sums of ten times the original annuity of £10, £15, £20 or £25 under deduction of any sum which the widow, if she survived her husband but died within ten years, had received. In addition, if an existing contributor died without leaving a widow but leaving a child or children under 18 years, such child or children equally were to receive an annuity, according to their father's rate of £27, £29, £30 or £32. For future contributors the provisions for children were to be (a) if the contributor, being a widower, died leaving a child or children under 18 an annuity equal to the widow's annuity; and (b) if the contributor left a widow an annuity equal to one-half of the widow's annuity increasing to equal the widow's annuity in the event of her death. On a vacancy in a benefice, vacant stipend was to be levied and collected. An actuarial valuation was to be carried out at least once every seven years. Any surplus could be applied, to the extent of not more than two-thirds in additions to the widows' annuities and childrens' provisions. The trustees were empowered to reduce the annuities but, if these fell below the levels at the commencement of the Order—£41, £49, £57 and £65—any reduction was to be applied equally and not in proportion to rates paid. The trustees were also empowered to vary the rates but not to reduce them below the then current level.

The *Church of Scotland Ministers' and Scottish University Professors' Widows' Fund (Amendment) Order Confirmation Act 1926* (**16 & 17 GEO. V—SESSION** 1926) amended the Order of 1923 on the narrative that, following upon the enactment of the Church of Scotland (Property and Endowments) Act 1925, the machinery provided by the Order of 1923 for collection of vacant stipend had ceased or would cease to be adequate. The amending Order provided that vacant stipend should continue to be payable to the Fund but collectable by the General Trustees provided that, in the case of any benefice remaining vacant for a longer period than six months, the vacant stipend accruing after the six-month period should be retainable by the General Trustees.

*The *Churches and Universities (Scotland) Widows' and Orphans' Fund Order Confirmation Act 1930* (ACT 20 & 21 GEO. 5 CH CXXXIV) confirmed a Provisional Order which repealed the Orders of 1923 and 1926

The Order proceeded on a narrative that the Church of Scotland and the United Free Church of Scotland were united under the name of "the Church of Scotland" by Acts of the General Assemblies of the Churches held on 1st and 2nd October 1929 and that it was expedient to amalgamate the Church of Scotland Ministers' and Scottish Professors' Widows' Fund and the Free Churches (Scotland) Widows' and Orphans' Fund. The Order further narrated that the Church of Scotland Fund was entitled, where a parish became vacant, to vacant stipend which right was modified by the Order of 1926; and that the Church of Scotland General Trustees, under the provisions of the Church of Scotland (Property and Endowments) Act 1925, were now entitled to receive all vacant stipend, subject to the modified rights of the said Fund and that it had been agreed that all vacant stipend should be collected by the General Trustees and paid by them to the Committee of the Maintenance of the Ministry fund, and that in full satisfaction of the Fund's right to vacant stipend there should be paid to the Fund from the Maintenance of the Ministry fund the sum of £140,000 payable in instalments of £3500 per annum for forty years without interest except on payments in arrear.

Accordingly the Order provided for the Church of Scotland Fund, the Free Churches Fund and all other property and assets vested in the trustees by the Order to constitute a Fund to be called the "Churches and Universities (Scotland) Widows' and Orphans' Fund."

The Order provided for payment to the Fund from the Church of Scotland Maintenance of the Ministry fund, the Free Church Sustentation fund or Church College funds of seven pounds per annum in respect of each minister, college professor or missionary, and also in respect of each vacant charge. A similar sum was also to be paid by each professor (not being a Church College professor) appointed to an office.

The Order provided for entry money to be paid at the rate of £10 if the minister, professor or missionary was at the time of induction or admission not more than 35 years of age, and otherwise of £15 and marriage-tax on the first and every subsequent marriage at the rate of £5 plus £1 for every year by which the age of the minister, professor or missionary exceeded that of his wife.

The Fund was to be administered by twenty trustees of whom twelve were to be ministers, professors or elders of the Church of Scotland, four were to be ministers, professors or elders of the Free Church of Scotland and four were to be professors of the universities. The trustees were to be a body corporate under the name and style of the "Churches and Universities (Scotland) Widows' and Orphans' Fund." They were authorised to invest in securities specified in the Trusts (Scotland) Act 1921 or available to trustees under subsequent legislation with further limited powers including investment in stock of any bank in Scotland incorporated by Royal Charter or Act of Parliament and in rents or income charged on lands in Great Britain.

The provisions in favour of widows of contributors at 22nd November 1923 to the Church of Scotland Ministers' and Scottish University Professors' Widows' Fund, i.e. annuities of £43, £52, £61 or £72 depending on the deceased husband's level of contribution, were preserved as were the rights of children of deceased contributors to capital sums of ten times the widow's annuity calculated on the original scale of £10, £15, £20 or £25 less any sum received by the contributor's widow in the event of her surviving him but dying within ten years of his death (to which capital sum was added, in the case of a contributor dying without leaving a widow but survived by a child or children under the age of eighteen, an annuity of £29, £32, £34 or £37 depending on the deceased's rate of contribution). The children of contributors who became contributors between 22nd November 1923 and the appointed date under the Order (2nd February

1929) were to receive, if under the age of eighteen and there being no widow, an annual family provision equal to the amount of the annuity to which the deceased contributor's widow, had he been survived by a widow, would have been entitled; in the event of a widow's annuity being payable, the children were to receive an annual family provision equal to one-half of the widow's annuity, increasing to equal the amount of the widow's annuity in the event of her death.

Widows, other than those referred to above, were to receive annuities of £64, while each child under eighteen years of age was to receive an annuity of £32 increased to £48 if there was no widow.

It was provided that whatever amount might be fixed from time to time as the widow's annuity, the annuity payable to a child during the lifetime of the widow should always be equal to fifty per cent of that amount increasing to seventy five per cent on the death of the widow.

Rules were laid down for increase or diminution of annuities to widows and children in the event of an actuarial investigation disclosing a capital surplus or deficiency.

The trustees were required annually to lay before the General Assemblies of the Churches and the university court of each of the Universities a report of the state and progress of the Fund.

*The *Churches and Universities (Scotland) Widows' and Orphans' Fund Order Confirmation Act, 1954* (ACT 2 & 3 ELIZ. 2 CH. LVII) confirmed a Provisional Order which repealed and substantially re-enacted with amendments the Order of 1930.

The trustees (consisting as before) were re-incorporated under the name of "The Trustees of the Churches and Universities (Scotland) Widows' and Orphans' Fund."

The provisions as to payment to the Fund from the Maintenance of the Ministry fund of the Church of Scotland, the Sustentation fund of the Free Church of Scotland, or the funds of the Free Church colleges, of seven pounds per annum for each minister or professor with power to the Trustees to increase such annual sum as also payment of such sum for every vacant charge or college charge were, re-enacted.

The provisions as to collection by the General Trustees of vacant stipend, payment thereof (less commission for collection) to the Maintenance of the Ministry fund and compensation therefor to the Fund (£3500 per annum for forty years) as provided in the Order of 1930 were similarly re-enacted.

Entry money was fixed, according to the age at admission, as follows:

not more than 35 years of age	£10
more than 35 but not more than 45 years of age	£15
more than 45 but not more than 55 years of age	£20
more than 55 years of age	£30

Marriage-tax was confirmed at £5 per marriage, plus £1 for each complete year by which the minister's or professor's age exceeded that of his wife.

The provisions for widows of contributors at 2nd October 1929 were effectively as in the Order of 1930, the annuities being stated to be "as increased or diminished from time to time by the Trustees." The provisions for the children under the age of 18 of such contributors were to be as in the Order of 1930, save that the annuity provisions, instead of being at the fixed rates of £29, £32, £34 or £37 were to be "of such amount as shall be equal to the annuity which would have been payable to their father's widow . . . under deduction of the sum of £14, £20, £27 or £33 respectively." The provisions for children of contributors who became contributors between 22nd November 1923 and 2nd October 1929 were to be as in the Order of 1930.

Annuities "'at the current rate" were to be paid to widows and to each of the children under 18 of ministers, professors or missionaries then or thereafter holding a charge or office. "Annuity at the current rate" was defined as meaning "an annuity of the amount specified in the repealed Order . . . as increased or diminished . . . by the Trustees under the powers conferred on them by this Order."

The investment powers of the trustees were greatly widened to include trustee investments according to the law of Scotland or the law of England, heritable property in Scotland, government stocks of the United Kingdom or Her

Majesty's dominions or protectorates or the United States of America and securities or stocks or shares including ordinary stocks or shares of any company incorporated in the United Kingdom or Her Majesty's dominions or protectorates or the United States of America.

The *Churches and Universities (Scotland) Widows' and Orphans' Fund (Amendment) Order Confirmation Act 1967* (ELIZ. II 1967 CH. XV) was enacted in the light of the changed circumstances with regard to remuneration and superannuation of professors and the establishment in Scotland of additional universities as a result of which it was no longer necessary for provision to be made under the Fund for widows and children of professors.

It was provided that the Order of 1954 should not apply to persons thereafter appointed as professors in any of the four universities. Professors, already members of the Fund, were given the option of withdrawing and receiving a refund of payments made by them.

The *Churches and Universities (Scotland) Widows' and Orphans' Fund (Amendment) Order Confirmation Act 1981* (ELIZ. II 1981 CH. II) referred to the important changes brought about by the Finance Act 1970 and subsequent legislation with respect to occupational pension schemes which made it expedient to amend the terms of the Fund so that it might be approved for tax treatment under Chapter II of Part II of the Finance Act 1970.

Accordingly, the trustees were empowered to transfer the interest of any beneficiary of the Fund to any other scheme approved under the Finance Act 1970. They were also empowered to discontinue the Fund should they consider it expedient and the rules for applying the assets in such event were set out. Limitations were imposed on the total pension which could be paid to any beneficiary under the Fund and any other scheme established by "the Employer" (defined to mean the church or university by which the member was employed).

Changes in the ministry were reflected in the amendment of the definition of "minister" in the Order of 1954 by removal of the words "(not being a woman)." It was provided that, "Any female person who on 5th April was an ordained minister in the employment of the churches shall have the option of not becoming a Member"; and further that, "Rates payable in respect of any female Member shall be determined by the Trustees." This Act provided that members not in the service of the Churches were to cease contributing and contributions for members were to cease at age 65.

The trustees were given extended investment powers.

The Fund now operates under the Act of 1954 as amended by the Acts of 1967 and 1981.

APPENDIX 2

The Church of Scotland Ministers' War Memorial and Orphan Funds

A Ian Dunlop TD MA BD

Closely related to, and in one sense a daughter of, the Church's Widows' and Orphans' Fund is the Ministers' War Memorial and Orphan Funds.

The Widows' Fund Act of Parliament of 1744 made provision for fatherless children of ministers. If a minister died not leaving a widow, the children were to receive a sum equalling ten years' annuities which would have been payable to the widow, had she lived, equally divided between them. If the widow should die or remarry before ten years elapsed after the commencement of the annuity, the children under sixteen should have the balance of the ten year's annuities still unpaid, equally divided among them.

By 1835, cases had occurred where fatherless children over sixteen had no provision for them and where widows had died soon after their husbands and before they had become entitled to annuities. In that year, the General Assembly agreed to establish a *Supplementary Orphan Fund* (see p 81) for (1) families all over sixteen years of age at the death of the father or remarriage of the mother and (2) families if the widow died or remarried before being entitled to ten year's annuities. (Payments were only made in May and November.) It was thought that a capital of £1500 would be required for the first purpose and by 1857 this sum had been raised. Provisions under the first purpose then took effect. For the attainment of both purposes, it was thought that a capital of £10,000 would be required, but this figure was never reached.

Membership of this scheme was open to all Widows' Fund Contributors who made a single payment of one guinea. In 1858 after the first treasurer, Alexander Webster of Aberdeen (the need for action had first been recognised in the Synod of Aberdeen in 1830) died, the fund was handed over to the Trustees of the Church's Widows' Fund for investment and administration gratuitously, the interest being the same as that earned from the "New Fund" investments of the Widows' Fund. Vigorous efforts were made to secure donations and to persuade ministers to pay the guinea. By 1859 the capital reached £2000. By 1889 there were only 251 contributors. In 1891 the capital was £5965, little more than half the desired amount.

In 1902 the General Assembly appointed a Committee to enquire into the whole matter. The Convener was a distinguished Edinburgh lawyer, Horatio R Macrae. This Committee reported in 1906 and the Assembly resolved (1) that in the case of new contributors, Supplementary Fund provisions should not in future be paid to families when all children were over twenty-five years of age at the time of the widow's death or remarriage, (2) that the second purpose of the Fund should come into effect for all contributors who signified their consent before the end of 1906, and for all new contributors and (3) that a new Orphan Fund should be created, with trustees who would provide £10 per annum to all fatherless children until they attained eighteen years of age. Horatio Macrae was appointed Convener and Chairman and in 1907 regulations were approved. It was thought that £40,000 would be required but an appeal was to be issued by the Supplementary Fund for £20,000 in the first instance, for the new Fund. The response at first was disappointing, but a generous gift from a Mr J D Nimmo of Glasgow meant that by 1913 the Orphan Fund Capital stood at £3000.

The General Assembly of the Church of Scotland heard that a letter had been received from "a country minister" pleading for a fund to provide for the maintenance and education of children of ministers who had lost their fathers in the War. The Assembly decided to "reconstitute the Orphan Fund to be a Memorial to the Ministers who had fallen on the field of battle", the young children of whom were to be the first beneficiaries. Other ministers and elders were asked to join the trustees to raise funds and local groups were formed. Thereafter for many years this "Committee" met each year before the Assembly and the Trustees reported to the Committee before reporting to the Assembly. Few, other than trustees, attended but the practice continued until 1965. The Orphan Fund in 1918 became *The Ministers' War Memorial and Orphan Fund*.

In 1925 the funds of the Supplementary Orphans' Fund were merged with those of the War Memorial and Orphan Fund to form the *Church of Scotland Ministers' War Memorial and Orphan Funds*. £13,061 was handed over to make a total of £17,615 capital. The funds were kept separate because of obligations to contributors. Only in 1962 were they brought together in one set of accounts.

The Capital of the "Funds" is now (1990) £34,072 invested in fixed interest stocks and in the Church of Scotland Trust. In 1990 £3985 was disbursed. The fund gives grants to orphans of ministers under the age of 21. From 1927 until 1944 there was a Chairman and also a Chairman of Trustees.

Chairmen

Horatio R Macrae WS	
Resigned 1926 Died 1930	1902
Professor (later Principal) William Fulton DD	1926–1952

Chairmen of Trustees

Sir C N Johnston (Lord Sands)	1930–1934
Sir William Chree, K.C.	1934–1936
Lord Wark	1936–1944
Rev. T B Stewart Thomson DD (Trustee 1948)	1952–1963
Lord Strachan (Trustee 1938)	1963–1976
Rev. A Ian Dunlop (Trustee 1955)	1976–1986
Lord Davidson (Trustee 1973)	1986–

Clerks and Treasurers

A W Russell WS (Hon)	1911
F P Milligan WS (Died 1961)	1919–1959
L R S MacKenzie WS	1959–1976
A L Bradley FAAI	
(Clerk to Widows' and Orphans' Fund)	1976–1983
Eric Hubbard LPFA	
(Clerk to Widows' and Orphans' Fund)	1984–

APPENDIX 3

Special Trust Funds
administered by the Trustees

One of the important duties of the Trustees is to see that all the widows have, from all sources, as good an income as possible. Each year a figure is declared, up to which the Trustees will make a grant from benevolent funds at their discretion.

In recent years, in addition, a Christmas gift has been sent to all widows. Gifts and legacies for this purpose, designated for benevolent purposes, are always most welcome, as are gifts and legacies for The Churches and Universities (Scotland) Widows' and Orphans' Fund, in which case they will be added to the capital of the Fund, which provides the annuities. The Special Trusts administered by the Trustees are as follows:

The Centesima Fund: Began 1688, see chapter 1. Grants to widows/orphans of deceased ministers of the pre-1690 diocese of Edinburgh—Capital c £1703.

Dr James Grant's Bequest: Revenue to widow/family of deceased contributor (not more than two years in succession) —Capital c £160

Mrs Mackay's Fund: Annuities to children of deceased ministers, over 18 years, with preference to blind or disabled in body or mind—Capital c £1222

Mrs Agnes McClymont's Bequest: Revenue for not more than three widows of ministers under lowest grade of Fund for maintenance of children and/or education, etc. Not more than three years—Capital c £362.

Mrs Matilda R Falconer's Bequest: Interest to widows whose total income is less than £160—Capital c £356.

The Cox-Leck Bequest: For widows and orphans of Church of Scotland—Capital c £9 920.

Rev Alexander Gray's Fund: For widows and orphans of Church of Scotland—Capital vested in Church of Scotland General Trustees Income c £1675.

The William Scott Bequest: For widows of ministers of the Church of Scotland—Capital c £20,711.

Church of Scotland Distribution Fund: Solely for widows of ministers of the Church of Scotland—Income c £19 067; used for Christmas Bonus.

Special Donations Fund and Miss D M Kirkwood's Bequest: Donations an legacies used to assist widows of those connected with the Fund, as testator or donor requires—Capital c £502.

Mrs J T Cox Fund: For widows and daughters of ministers of Church of Scotland—Capital vested in Mrs J T Cox Trustees; Income c £2685.

Mrs Butler's Trust: Grants to widows and dependent relatives of ministers of Church of Scotland—Capital vested in Presbytery of Edinburgh; Income c £525.

Mrs Dobie's Trust: Grants to widows and orphans of ministers of Church of Scotland—Capital vested in Presbytery of Edinburgh; Income c £283.

Rev Robert Ferguson's Bequest: Grants to dependants of ministers of Church of Scotland—Capital c £29,873.

The Manse Fellowship Trust: For widows and orphans of the Church of Scotland—Capital c £4821.

In recent years the Trustees have received the benefit of a covenanted gift from *The Church of Scotland Fire Insurance Trust*, for which they are most grateful.

APPENDIX 4

Papers and Books

The minutes of the Trustees and the records of the Fund are kept at the Scottish Record Office in Edinburgh (Ref. CH9 1-25).

Recent material and some old papers are kept at the Office of the Fund at 121 George Street, Edinburgh.

New College Library, Edinburgh, has some copies of reports and records.

Other publications of interest:

Alexander Mackie: *Facile Princeps*, 1956. This is the history of the beginning of life insurance in America, in particular the Presbyterian Ministers' Fund. It contains an excellent survey of the early Scottish Fund.

David Deuchar: *Notes on Widows' Funds*, transactions of the Actuarial Society of Scotland, vol 3, p 61, 1894.

'Fiasco', the Magazine of Staple Inn Actuarial Society, 1987, No 93, articles by Chris Lewin.

See also Robert Wallace, predecessor of Malthus, and the pioneering Actuary Mary Pickard Winsor.